TEACHER'S PET PUBLICATIONS

LITPLAN TEACHER PACK
for
Tuck Everlasting
based on the book by
Natalie Babbitt

Written by
Janine H. Sherman

© 1997 Teacher's Pet Publications
All Rights Reserved

This **LitPlan** for Natalie Babbitt's
Tuck Everlasting
has been brought to you by Teacher's Pet Publications, Inc.

Copyright Teacher's Pet Publications 1997
11504 Hammock Point
Berlin MD 21811

Only the student materials in this unit plan (such as worksheets, study questions, and tests) may be reproduced multiple times for use in the purchaser's classroom.

TABLE OF CONTENTS - *Tuck Everlasting*

Introduction	5
Unit Objectives	8
Reading Assignment Sheet	9
Unit Outline	10
Study Questions (Short Answer)	13
Quiz/Study Questions (Multiple Choice)	21
Pre-reading Vocabulary Worksheets	37
Lesson One (Introductory Lesson)	53
Nonfiction Assignment Sheet	60
Oral Reading Evaluation Form	56
Writing Assignment 1	58
Writing Assignment 2	69
Writing Assignment 3	72
Writing Evaluation Form	67
Vocabulary Review Activities	82
Extra Writing Assignments/Discussion ?s	74
Unit Review Activities	84
Unit Tests	87
Unit Resource Materials	129
Vocabulary Resource Materials	147

A FEW NOTES ABOUT THE AUTHOR
NATALIE BABBITT

BABBITT, Natalie (1932-   ). Natalie Babbitt was born and grew up in Dayton, Ohio. In her youth she liked to read fairy tales and myths, but her favorite hobby was to draw. She received early art lessons, seen to by her portrait-painting mother, and wanted only to be an illustrator. After graduating from Smith College, where she specialized in art, she married Samuel Babbitt, an academic administrator. She spent the next ten years raising their three children born between 1956 and 1960.

In 1966 she and her husband decided to collaborate on a children's book, *The Forty-Ninth Magician*. Following that joint venture, Mr. Babbitt was named president of Kirkland College in Clinton, New York. Finding herself without a writer, Mrs. Babbitt decided to try writing on her own, and now finds that though she still enjoys illustrating, she finds writing is equally challenging and satisfying.

Believing she could do best with rhyme in the beginning, she wrote her first two books, *Dick Foote and the Shark* and *Phoebe's Revolt*, in verse. Next came *The Search for the Delicious*, which is rooted in all the fairy tales she read as a child. *Kneeknock Rise* and *Goody Hall*, two of her novels were next with *The Something*, a picture book, falling in between.

She has continued to illustrate for others, as well as herself. She has written and illustrated two books of stories about the devil called *The Devil's Storybook* and *The Devil's Other Storybook*. Three novels were written in between those two: *Tuck Everlasting*, the modern classic which explores the possibility that endless life may be more of a curse than a blessing; a seashore fantasy/love story, *The Eyes of the Amaryllis* and *Herbert Rowbarge,* the story of a man who never knows he has a twin brother. Her first full color picture book, *Nellie: A Cat on Her Own* has received professional praise calling it a charming fantasy with the same graceful and precise language as *Tuck Everlasting*. Natalie Babbitt, a descendent of Zane Grey and the grandmother of three, lives in Providence, Rhode Island.

INTRODUCTION - *Tuck Everlasting*

This unit has been designed to develop students' reading, writing, thinking, and language skills through exercises and activities related to *Tuck Everlasting* by Natalie Babbitt. It includes twenty lessons, supported by extra resource materials.

The **introductory lesson** introduces students to the theme of the novel (everlasting life) through a cooperative learning activity. Following the introductory activity, students are given an explanation of how the activity relates to the book they are about to read. Following the transition, students are given the materials they will be using during the unit.

The **reading assignments** are approximately twenty pages each; some are a little shorter while others are a little longer. Students have approximately 15 minutes of pre-reading work to do prior to each reading assignment. This pre-reading work involves reviewing the study questions for the assignment and doing some vocabulary work for 10 vocabulary words they will encounter in their reading.

The **study guide questions** are fact-based questions; students can find the answers to these questions right in the text. These questions come in two formats: short answer or multiple choice. The best use of these materials is probably to use the short answer version of the questions as study guides for students (since answers will be more complete), and to use the multiple choice version for occasional quizzes. It might be a good idea to make transparencies of your answer keys for the overhead projector.

The **vocabulary work** is intended to enrich students' vocabularies as well as to aid in the students' understanding of the book. Prior to each reading assignment, students will complete a two-part worksheet for 10 vocabulary words in the upcoming reading assignment. Part I focuses on students' use of general knowledge and contextual clues by giving the sentence in which the word appears in the text. Students are then to write down what they think the words mean based on the words' usage. Part II nails down the definitions of the words by giving students dictionary definitions of the words and having students match the words to the correct definitions based on the words' contextual usage. Students should then have an understanding of the words when they meet them in the text.

After each reading assignment, students will go back and formulate answers for the study guide questions. Discussion of these questions serves as a **review** of the most important events and ideas presented in the reading assignments.

After students complete extra discussion questions, there is a **vocabulary review** lesson which pulls together all of the fragmented vocabulary lists for the reading assignments and gives students a review of all of the words they have studied.

Following the reading of the book, two lessons are devoted to the **extra discussion questions/writing assignments/activities**. These questions focus on interpretation, critical analysis and personal response, employing a variety of thinking skills and adding to the students' understanding of the novel. These questions are done as a **group activity**. Using the information they have acquired so far through individual work and class discussions, students get together to further examine the text and to brainstorm ideas relating to the themes of the novel.

The group activity is followed by a **reports and discussion/ activity** session in which the groups share their ideas about the book with the entire class; thus, the entire class gets exposed to many different ideas regarding the themes and events of the book.

There are three **writing assignments** in this unit, each with the purpose of informing, persuading, or having students express personal opinions. The first assignment gives students the opportunity to express their personal ideas: students will defend their choice about whether to drink or not to drink from the spring that grants eternal life. The second assignment is to inform: students will create an advertisement that the man in the yellow suit might have used to sell the spring water. The third assignment is to give students a chance to persuade: students will pretend to be either Mae's defense or prosecuting attorney and present their closing remarks to the jury at her trial.

In addition, there is a **nonfiction reading assignment**. Students are required to read a piece of nonfiction related in some way to *Tuck Everlasting*. After reading their nonfiction pieces, students will fill out a worksheet on which they answer questions regarding facts, interpretation, criticism, and personal opinions. During one class period, students make **oral presentations** about the nonfiction pieces they have read. This not only exposes all students to a wealth of information, it also gives students the opportunity to practice **public speaking**.

There is an optional **class project** (The Treegap Times) through which students will have the opportunity to contribute to the compilation of a class newspaper.

The **review lesson** pulls together all of the aspects of the unit. The teacher is given four or five choices of activities or games to use which all serve the same basic function of reviewing all of the information presented in the unit.

The **unit test** comes in two formats: all multiple choice-matching-true/false or with a mixture of matching, short answer, and composition. As a convenience, two different tests for each format have been included.

There are additional **support materials** included with this unit. The **unit resource section** includes suggestions for an in-class library, crossword and word search puzzles related to the novel, and extra vocabulary games and worksheets. There is a list of **bulletin board ideas** which gives the teacher suggestions for bulletinboards to go along with this unit.

In addition, there is a list of **extra class activities** the teacher could choose from to enhance the unit or as a substitution for an exercise the teacher might feel is inappropriate for his/her class. **Answer keys** are located directly after the **reproducible student materials** throughout the unit. The student materials may be reproduced for use in the teacher's classroom without infringement of copyrights. No other portion of this unit may be reproduced without the written consent of Teacher's Pet Publications, Inc.

UNIT OBJECTIVES - *Tuck Everlasting*

1. Through reading Natalie Babbitt's *Tuck Everlasting*, students will be introduced to the concept of eternal life.

2. Students will be able to differentiate between characters as protagonist or antagonist.

3. Students will be able to recognize the genre of fantasy.

4. Students will gain appreciation for and demonstrate proficiency in identifying and using figurative language.

5. Students will demonstrate their understanding of the text on four levels: factual, interpretive, critical and personal.

6. Students will be given the opportunity to practice reading aloud and silently to improve their skills in each area.

7. Students will answer questions to demonstrate their knowledge and understanding of the main events and characters in *Tuck Everlasting* as they relate to the author's theme development.

8. Students will enrich their vocabularies and improve their understanding of the novel through the vocabulary lessons prepared for use in conjunction with the novel.

9. The writing assignments in this unit are geared to several purposes:
    a. To have students demonstrate their abilities to inform, to persuade, or to express their own personal ideas
        Note: Students will demonstrate ability to write effectively to <u>inform</u> by developing and organizing facts to convey information. Students will demonstrate the ability to write effectively to <u>persuade</u> by selecting and organizing relevant information, establishing an argumentative purpose, and by designing an appropriate strategy for an identified audience. Students will demonstrate the ability to write effectively to <u>express personal ideas</u> by selecting a form and its appropriate elements.
    b. To check the students' reading comprehension
    c. To make students think about the ideas presented by the novel
    d. To encourage logical thinking
    e. To provide an opportunity to practice good grammar and improve students' use of the English language.

10. Students will read aloud, report, and participate in large and small group discussions to improve their public speaking and personal interaction skills.

READING ASSIGNMENT SHEET - *Tuck Everlasting*

Date Assigned	Reading Assignment (Chapters)	Completion Date
	Prologue-Chapter 4	
	Chapters 5-8	
	Chapters 9-13	
	Chapters 14-18	
	Chapters 19-22	
	Chapters 23-Epilogue	

UNIT OUTLINE - *Tuck Everlasting*

1 Introduction Materials PVR Prologue-Ch. 4	2 Study ? Prologue-Ch. 4 PVR Ch. 5-8	3 Read Ch. 5-8 Oral Reading Evaluation	4 Study? Ch. 5-8 Writing Assignment #1	5 Nonfiction Reading PVR Ch. 9-13
6 Study ? Ch. 9-13 PVR Ch. 14-18	7 Study ? Ch. 14-18 PV Ch. 19-22	8 Figurative Language	9 Read Ch. 19-22 Writing Conference	10 Study ? Ch. 19-22 Writing Assignment #2
11 Work Session Ads PV Ch. 23-Epilogue	12 Read Ch. 23-Epilogue Protagonist/Antagonist	13 Study? Ch. 23-Epilogue Writing Assignment #3	14 Extra Discussion Questions	15 Extra Discussion Questions
16 Share Nonfiction & Writing Assignments	17 Vocabulary Review	18 Review	19 Test	20 Project

Key: P = Preview Study Questions   V = Vocabulary Work   R = Read

STUDY GUIDE QUESTIONS

SHORT ANSWER STUDY QUESTIONS - *Tuck Everlasting*

Prologue- Chapter 4
1. Which month is at the top of the live-long year?
2. Describe the touch-me-not cottage.
3. Why did the wood 'make you want to speak in whispers'?
4. What lies at the center of the wood?
5. Where does Mae Tuck tell her husband she is going that morning at dawn?
6. What item does Mae take along with her?
7. For how many years had all the Tucks remained exactly the same?
8. What does Winnie Foster tell a toad at noon the same day?
9. Why does she want to do this?
10. Describe the stranger who appears at the Foster's gate at sunset of the same day.
11. Why has he come?
12. Why did Winnie's grandmother become so excited when she heard music coming from the wood?

Chapters 5-8
1. Why did Winnie awaken disheartened the next morning?
2. Where does Winnie decide to go?
3. What does Winnie see there?
4. What does Winnie want to do that the boy refuses to allow her to do?
5. How was Winnie's kidnapping different from her imagined one?
6. What calmed Winnie's sobbing?
7. When did the Tucks realize there was something peculiar about themselves and their horse?
8. Why did Miles' wife leave him and take the children?
9. What conclusion did the Tucks draw concerning their changelessness?
10. How do Jesse and Miles' opinions differ about their predicament?
11. Who secretly overheard the entire Tuck story?

Chapters 9-13
1. Describe the Tuck homeplace.
2. How does Angus Tuck react to his family bringing Winnie home with them?
3. How is the Tuck home different from what Winnie is used to?
4. How do Angus and Mae make a living?
5. Where do the boys go when they leave home and what do they do?
6. When is Mae certain her boys will show up at home?
7. How does Winnie feel during dinner at the Tucks?
8. Why does Angus take Winnie out in the rowboat on the pond?
9. What news does Miles bring at the end of chapter 12?

Short Answer Study Guide Questions - *Tuck Everlasting* Page 2

Chapters 14-18
1. What suggestion does Jesse make to Winnie?
2. How is Winnie feeling before she falls asleep that night?
3. What is the man in the yellow suit asking as a trade from the Fosters for the return of their daughter?
4. How do the constable and the stranger get along on the ride to the Tucks?
5. Where does Miles take Winnie the next morning?
6. What does Miles share with Winnie about his future goals?
7. Retell the quote that Miles tells Winnie after throwing the fish back into the pond.
8. How have Winnie's feelings changed about the Tucks?
9. Who comes knocking at the door at the end of chapter 18?

Chapters 19-22
1. How did the stranger come to know of the "ageless" family?
2. Explain the stranger's plan for the wood.
3. What does Mae do that surprises everyone?
4. How does Winnie protect the Tucks when the constable accuses them of kidnaping?
5. Why does Winnie think Mae Tuck can't be hanged?
6. How do the Fosters react upon Winnie's return?
7. What news does the constable bring the Fosters?
8. Before falling asleep that night what does Winnie vow she must do?
9. For what reason does Winnie ask her grandmother for some water the next day?
10. Who appears at the Foster's gate and what is his plan?
11. How does Winnie offer to help the Tucks?

Chapters 23- Epilogue
1. How is Winnie feeling in the three hours before she is to meet Jesse?
2. How is Miles able to help his mother?
3. Just as Mae gets out of the window, what happens?
4. What does Winnie do after Mae gets out?
5. What caused the loud crash during the night at the jailhouse?
6. How did the constable react when he found out about the switch?
7. How did Winnie's status change with her peers because of the incident?
8. Explain what Winnie does to the toad and why.
9. When the Tucks returned, how had Treegap changed?
10. What do the Tucks learn happened to the wood, tree, and spring?
11. Why does Mae state they have no need to come back to Treegap?
12. How many years had passed since that first week in August with Winnie when the Tucks returned?
13. What do Mae and Angus see in the road before leaving Treegap?

ANSWER KEY SHORT ANSWER STUDY QUESTIONS - *Tuck Everlasting*

Prologue- Chapter 4

1. Which month is at the top of the live-long year?
    The first week of August hangs at the very top of the live-long year.

2. Describe the touch-me-not cottage.
    It was a square and solid cottage with a touch-me-not appearance surrounded by grass cut painfully to the quick and enclosed by a capable iron fence some four feet high which clearly said "Move on-we don't want you here." It was so proud of itself that you wanted to make a lot of noise as you passed, maybe even throw a rock or two.

3. Why did the wood 'make you want to speak in whisper'?
    It had a sleeping appearance, otherworld appearance that made you want to speak in whispers. This, at least is what the cows must have thought: "Let it keep its peace *we* won't disturb it."

4. What lies at the center of the wood?
    A giant ash tree lies at the center of the wood with a bubbling spring among its roots with a pile of pebbles piled there to conceal it.

5. Where does Mae Tuck tell her husband she is going that morning at dawn?
    She is going to take the horse and ride down to the wood to meet her sons.

6. What item did Mae take along with her?
    She took the one pretty thing she owned: her music box, painted with roses and lilies of the valley.

7. For how many years had all the Tucks remained exactly the same?
    For eighty-seven years they had all remained exactly the same.

8. What does Winnie Foster tell a toad at noon the same day?
    She wants to be by herself for a change. She wants to do something that would make some kind of difference in the world. She wants to run away from home.

9. Why does she want to do this?
    She is closely watched constantly by her parents and grandfather with very little freedom.

10. Describe the stranger who appears at the Foster's gate at sunset of the same day.
    He was remarkably tall and narrow with a long chin that faded off into a thin, apologetic beard. His suit was a jaunty yellow that seemed to glow a little in the fading light. A black hat dangled from one hand.

Tuck Everlasting Study Guide Question Answers page 2

11. Why has he come?
    He's looking for a family

12. Why did Winnie's grandmother become so excited when she heard music coming from the wood?
    She thinks it is the elf music she had heard long ago. She had told Winnie stories about it.

Chapters 5-8

1. Why did Winnie awaken disheartened the next morning?
   She was annoyed at herself for being afraid to run away after all.

2. Where does Winnie decide to go?
   She decides to go into the wood to see if she can discover what or who had made the music the night before.

3. What does Winnie see there?
   She sees a thin, sunburned wonderful boy drinking from a little spring near a huge tree.

4. What does Winnie want to do that the boy refuses to allow her to do?
   She wants to take a drink from the little spring from which she saw him drinking.

5. How was Winnie's kidnapping different from her imagined one?
   Her kidnappers appeared as alarmed as she was.

6. What calmed Winnie's sobbing?
   She ceased sobbing after Mae started her music box.

7. When did the Tucks realize there was something peculiar about themselves and their horse?
   They realized something wasn't right when potentially harmful events didn't affect them.

8. Why did Miles' wife leave him and take the children?
   She thought he had sold his soul to the devil because he wasn't aging.

9. What conclusion did the Tucks draw concerning their changelessness?
   They decided that the source of their changelessness was the spring they had drunk from in the wood. The cat had not drunk from it and had died ten years earlier.

10. How do Jesse and Miles' opinions differ about their predicament?
    Jesse thinks you might as well enjoy it as along as you can't change it, while Miles is more serious about it.

Tuck Everlasting Study Guide Question Answers page 3

11. Who secretly overheard the entire Tuck story?
    The man in the yellow suit had crept up in the bushes and heard the entire fascinating story.

Chapters 9-13

1. Describe the Tuck homeplace.
    Their barn-red homely little house sits in a deep hollow below which is a tiny lake.

2. How does Angus Tuck react to his family bringing Winnie home with them?
    He thinks it is the finest thing to happen to them in eighty years.

3. How is the Tuck home different from what Winnie is used to?
    She has been trained to keep absolute order and their home was pleasantly cluttered and is in a state of disarray.

4. How do Angus and Mae make a living?
    They make things to sell like wooden toys and utensils.

5. Where do the boys go when they leave home and what do they do?
    They go to different places, find odd jobs, and try to bring home some of their money.

6. When is Mae certain her boys will show up at home?
    They come home every ten years during the first week in August.

7. How does Winnie feel during dinner at the Tucks?
    Her spirits drop and she becomes homesick.

8. Why does Angus take Winnie out in the rowboat on the pond?
    He wants to explain to her the cycle of life as compared to the cycle of the water's life. He wants her to understand how horrible it really is to be outside of the cycle and STUCK like the Tucks. He stresses how dangerous it would be for others to discover the spring.

9. What news does Miles bring at the end of chapter 12?
    Someone has stolen the Tuck's horse.

Chapters 14-18

1. What suggestion does Jesse make to Winnie?
    He asks her to wait six years, when she will be his age, and then drink from the spring. They can then marry, see the world, and have a grand time.

Tuck Everlasting Study Guide Question Answers page 4

2. How is Winnie feeling before she falls asleep that night?
    She is very confused, but feeling kindly towards the Tucks. She is worried about what her father will do when he finds them.

3. What is the man in the yellow suit asking as a trade from the Fosters for the return of their daughter?
    He wants to own the wood; signed over to him legally.

4. How do the constable and the stranger get along on the ride to the Tucks?
    The constable is a friendly, talkative man and the stranger is annoyed and rides ahead.

5. Where does Miles take Winnie the next morning?
    He takes her fishing.

6. What does Miles share with Winnie about his future goals?
    He tells her that someday he'll find a way to do something important.

7. Retell the quote that Miles tells Winnie after throwing the fish back into the pond.
    "People got to be meat-eaters sometimes, though. It's the natural way. And that means killing things."

8. How have Winnie's feelings changed about the Tucks?
    She loves this peculiar family and feels that they belong to her.

9. Who comes knocking at the door at the end of chapter 18?
    The man in the yellow suit is at the door of the Tucks.

Chapters 19-22
1. How did the stranger come to know of the "ageless" family?
    His grandmother had told him wild, unbelievable stories of an "odd" family. A dear friend of hers had married into this family and she and her two children had come to live with his grandmother for awhile. The tune from Mae's music box had been a clue, when the stranger had heard it at the Foster's gate he knew he was close to finding them.

2. Explain the stranger's plan for the wood.
    He plans to sell the water.

3. What does Mae do that surprises everyone?
    She hits the stranger in the back of his skull with the stock of Angus' shotgun.

Tuck Everlasting Study Guide Question Answers page 5

4. How does Winnie protect the Tucks when the constable accuses them of kidnapping?
    She tells him that they didn't kidnap her, she went with them because she wanted to.

5. Why does Winnie think Mae Tuck can't be hanged?
    She would not be able to hanged because they can't die.

6. How do the Fosters react upon Winnie's return?
    They seize her with weeping, hugging, fretting, and fussing.

7. What news does the constable bring the Fosters?
    He tells them that the fellar-the one they sold their land to-is dead.

8. Before falling asleep that night what does Winnie vow she must do?
    She knows she has to do something to help Mae.

9. For what reason does Winnie ask her grandmother for some water the next day?
    She wants to give some water to the toad because it so dry outside.

10. Who appears at the Foster's gate and what is his plan?
    Jesse appears and tells Winnie that Miles plans to take the window, bars and all, out of the jailhouse so Mae can climb out late that night.

11. How does Winnie offer to help the Tucks?
    She tells Jesse she will take Mae's place in the jailhouse after they get Mae out of the window, so they can get further away before the constable realizes his prisoner is gone.

Chapters 23- Epilogue
1. How is Winnie feeling in the three hours before she is to meet Jesse?
    She is feeling restless, excited, and guilty about leaving home again without permission.

2. How is Miles able to help his mother?
    He pried out all the nails from the window and yanked the window out of the jailhouse wall so she could climb out of it and escape.

3. Just as Mae gets out of the window, what happens?
    It begins to rain.

4. What does Winnie do after Mae gets out?
    Winnie climbs in the window and covers herself with the blanket to make herself look like Mae.

Tuck Everlasting Study Guide Question Answers page 6

5. What caused the loud crash during the night at the jailhouse?
    The gallows had blown over in the wind of the storm.

6. How did the constable react when he found out about the switch?
    He became very angry and called her a criminal and an accomplice. He released her into the custody of her parents because of her age,

7. How did Winnie's status change with her peers because of the incident?
    They were impressed by what she had done. She was a figure of romance to them now. They came by to look at her and to talk to her through the fence. Before she had been too clean to be a real friend.

8. Explain what Winnie does to the toad and why.
    She poured the precious water from the spring that Jesse had given to her over the toad so he would not have to be harmed by the dog. She wanted to protect him.

9. When the Tucks returned, how had Treegap changed?
    There were many other streets crossing over the main street and they were blacktopped. The wood and Winnie's cottage were gone. There were many shops and businesses, as well as a hotel and diner.

10. What do the Tucks learn happened to the wood, tree, and spring?
    They discover there was a big electrical storm. The big tree got hit by lightning, caught fire and had to be bulldozed out. All sign of the spring was gone.

11. Why does Mae state they have no need to come back to Treegap?
    They find Winnie's tombstone in the family plot at the local cemetery.

12. How many years had passed since that first week in August with Winnie when the Tucks returned?
    They say that Winnie had been dead for two years. Her inscription lists 1948 as the year of her death, which makes it 1950. Her year of birth was listed as 1870. She was 10 years old when they had been with her; so that would be 1880. The number of years from 1880 to 1950 is seventy years.

13. What do Mae and Angus see in the road before leaving Treegap?
    They see the everlasting toad Winnie poured the spring water over.

MULTIPLE CHOICE STUDY GUIDE/QUIZ QUESTIONS - *Tuck Everlasting*

Prologue- Chapter 4

1. The month at the top of the live-long year is
    a. January
    b. December
    c. August
    d. none of the above

2. The touch-me-not cottage seemed to say
    a. "Move on-we don't want you here."
    b. "Welcome one and all."
    c. " Go away and don't come back."
    d. " Please don't pick the daisies."

3. Why did the wood 'make you want to speak in whispers'?
    a. It was spooky due to the large, dark pine trees.
    b. The darkness scared the animals and made them quiet.
    c. The trees were so tall and dark.
    d. It had a sleeping appearance.

4. What lies at the center of the wood?
    a. an ash tree
    b. a pebble- covered spring
    c. a set of pine trees
    d. both a and b

5. Mae Tuck tells her husband that
    a. she is going to meet their sons at the wood.
    b. she needs a new dress to look better for the boys' visit.
    c. he needs to be more positive about their predicament.
    d. they should adopt another child.

6. When Mae leaves for her journey, she takes
    a. a music box painted with roses and lilies of the valley.
    b. the old family horse.
    c. the one pretty thing she owns.
    d. all of the above

Study Guide/Quiz Questions- *Tuck Everlasting* Multiple Choice Format Page 2

7. The Tucks have not changed for
    a. seventy years.
    b. sixty-five years.
    c. seventeen years.
    d. eighty-seven years.

8. What does Winnie Foster tell a toad at noon the same day?
    a. She wants to be by herself for a change.
    b. She wants to do something that would make some kind of difference in the world.
    c. She wants to run away from home.
    d. all of the above

9. Why does Winnie want to do this?
    a. She is closely watched constantly by her parents and grandfather with very little freedom.
    b. She reads lots of adventure books and has a vivid imagination.
    c. She is tired of never seeing her relatives who live in on the other side of the wood.
    d. She wants to change the world for the better because her parents encourage her to do it.

10. Describe the stranger who appears at the Foster's gate at sunset of the same day.
    a. He was remarkably tall with a round chin.
    b. He was tall and wore a yellow suit.
    c. He wore a black hat and had a thick mustache.
    d. He was tall and lanky with a light- colored suit and hat.

11. The stranger is looking for
    a. the lost tree and spring.
    b. Winnie's father, who owed the wood.
    c. a certain family he thought lived nearby.
    d. a friendly toad that he has been following.

12. Winnie's Grandmother thinks the music coming from the wood is the
    a. music of the elves of long ago.
    b. result of her lost music box.
    c. same music she heard the night before.
    d. the most beautiful thing she has ever heard.

Study Guide/Quiz Questions- *Tuck Everlasting* Multiple Choice Format Page 3

Chapters 5-8

1. Winnie awakens galled at herself the next morning because she
    a. is tired of her grandmother fussing over her.
    b. is afraid to run away after all.
    c. can't find her friend, the toad.
    d. doesn't want to go with her parents to church.

2. Winnie decides to
    a. go into the wood and look for the maker of the music she heard.
    b. run away and never come back to her overprotective parents.
    c. ask her parents if she can have a toad for a pet.
    d. go over to her best friend's house for the afternoon.

3. When she is in the wood, Winnie first sees
    a. a bubbling spring partially hidden by a stack of pebbles.
    b. a broken-down horse resting after its journey.
    c. a young brown- haired boy wearing green suspenders.
    d. a young curly-headed boy dressed in an elf suit.

4. Winnie wants to
    a. drink from the flowing stream.
    b. know where from where the stranger has come.
    c. be able to leave home whenever she wants
    d. drink from the bubbling water.

5. Winnie's kidnapping is similar to what she imagined it would be like.
    a. true
    b. false

6. Mae is able to calm Winnie's sobbing by
    a. hugging her close to herself.
    b. explaining that they are harmless and will take her home soon.
    c. winding up the music box and letting it play its melody.
    d. reassuring her the wood and the spring.

Study Guide/Quiz Questions- *Tuck Everlasting* Multiple Choice Format Page 4

7. The Tucks realized they were different from normal people when
    a. their cat died a natural death.
    b. they were not harmed by potentially harmful events.
    c. Miles wife left and took the children.
    d. none of the above

8. Miles wife left him and took the two children because
    a. she thought he had sold his soul to the devil.
    b. he wasn't aging like she was.
    c. she thought the whole family was witches or worse.
    d. all of the above

9. The Tucks came to the conclusion that
    a. the spring was the source of their agelessness.
    b. they were crazy.
    c. their cat was luckier than they.
    d. the T carved in the ash tree had not changed either.

10. Miles and Jesse feel the same about their fate.
    a. true
    b. false

11. Unbeknownest to Winnie, Mae, Jesse, and Miles; who overheard their entire unbelievable story?
    a. the Fosters
    b. the constable
    c. the man in the yellow suit
    d. Angus

Study Guide/Quiz Questions- *Tuck Everlasting* Multiple Choice Format Page 5

Chapters 9-13

1. The Tuck home is
    a. painted barn-red and has a tiny lake near it.
    b. deeper in the wood, past the spring.
    c. a yellow clapboard house in a clearing.
    d. none of the above

2. Angus Tuck's reaction upon his family bringing Winnie home with them is one of
    a. fear.
    b. elation.
    c. confusion.
    d. frustration.

3. The main difference between the Foster house and the Tuck's is
    a. the style in which they eat their meals.
    b. the way they greet each other.
    c. the lack of overall organization and order.
    d. the openness with which they share their feelings.

4. Angus and Mae are able to make a living by
    a. depending on Miles' income from his jobs.
    b. selling water from the spring.
    c. selling the fish they catch in the pond.
    d. making wooden toys and utensils and selling them.

5. When the boys are away from home they
    a. get odd jobs and try to save some of their pay.
    b. return to the same job and send home their checks.
    c. travel around to see the country and come back and report to their parents.
    d. none of the above

6. Miles and Jesse return home
    a. every ten years during the first week in August.
    b. whenever they get a chance.
    c. both a and b
    d. neither a nor b

Study Guide/Quiz Questions- *Tuck Everlasting* Multiple Choice Format Page 6

7. During dinner at the Tuck's Winnie
   a. gets a tummy ache and has to lie down.
   b. becomes homesick as her spirits drop.
   c. is amused at the Tuck's lack of manners.
   d. has a fit of hysterics and can't be settled.

8. Angus takes Winnie out in the rowboat after dinner to
   a. explain the danger of the spring water.
   b. use the water as an example of the cycle of life.
   c. express his frustration at being stuck in the life process.
   d. all of the above

9. At the end of the chapter Miles reveals that
   a. Winnie's parents have sent the constable to find her.
   b. the stranger has overheard their story and wants to negotiate.
   c. someone has stolen the family horse.
   d. he must go away to learn a new trade.

Study Guide/Quiz Questions - *Tuck Everlasting* Multiple Choice Format Page 7

Chapters 14-18

1. Jesse suggests to Winnie that she
    a. run away with him for a grand time.
    b. tell her parents why she left home.
    c. go fishing with him in the morning.
    d. drink from the spring when she is his age, marry him, and stay that age forever with him.

2. Before falling asleep, Winnie fears what her father will do to the Tucks.
    a. true
    b. false

3. The man in the yellow suit is asking
    a. directions to the Tuck household.
    b. Angus for permission to fish on his pond.
    c. for the wood to be signed over to him in return for Winnie.
    d. Winnie to come to Treegap with him for a church picnic.

4. The constable and the man in the yellow suit become fast friends.
    a. true
    b. false

5. The following morning, Miles takes Winnie
    a. horseback riding
    b. for a walk down by the pond.
    c. fishing.
    d. home to her parents.

6. What do Miles and Winnie have in common?
    a. Neither of them like to kill animals.
    b. They both are allergic to certain foods.
    c. They both are unhappy with how their parents treat them.
    d. Both want to do something important; to make a difference.

7. After Miles throws the rainbow trout back in the pond he tells Winnie
    a. that sometimes you have to kill; it's the natural way of things.
    b. his family will be sore because they were expecting fish for breakfast.
    c. she will come to like the looks of fish after awhile.
    d. he doesn't like to keep them either, they are too much trouble to clean.

Study Guide/Quiz Questions- *Tuck Everlasting* Multiple Choice Format Page 8

8. Winnie's feelings about the Tucks have changed since the kidnapping.
    a. true
    b. false

9. Who comes knocking at the Tuck's door at the end of the chapter 18?
    a. the constable looking for the girl.
    b. Winnie's parents.
    c. the man in the yellow suit.
    d. the next-door-neighbor returning the horse.

Study Guide/Quiz Questions- *Tuck Everlasting* Multiple Choice Format Page 9

Chapters 19-22

1. The man in the yellow suit learned of the "ageless" family through
    a. watching and waiting for them.
    b. his grandmother's friend.
    c. the music of Mae's music box.
    d. none of the above

2. What is the stranger's plan for the wood?
    a. He has an idea for a town park.
    b. He wants to build a set of new cottages.
    c. He plans to sell the water.
    d. He wants the Tucks to work for him running the ferris wheel.

3. When the stranger tried to take Winnie away against her will, Mae
    a. shot him with Angus' shotgun.
    b. hit him with the stock of Angus' rifle.
    c. grabbed Winnie away from him.
    d. cried for help from the approaching constable.

4. Winnie told the constable that the Tucks did not kidnap her; she went with them willingly.
    a. true
    b. false

5. Winnie knows that Mae must not be hanged because
    a. she will not be there to help her family.
    b. she loves her too much.
    c. she is not guilty of any wrongdoing.
    d. she can't die.

6. The Foster's reaction upon Winnie's homecoming was one of:
    a. fear, anxiety, and cheer.
    b. delight, anger, and curiosity.
    c. excitement, fretting, and relief.
    d. hysteria, question, punishment.

Study Guide/Quiz Questions- *Tuck Everlasting* Multiple Choice Format Page 10

7. The constable brings the Fosters news that
    a. the man in the yellow suit is dead.
    b. the man in the yellow suit is in critical condition.
    c. the stranger's family is waiting at the hospital for a report on his condition.
    d. Mae is under arrest for assault and battery.

8. Winnie vows that night before falling asleep that she must
    a. help Angus release Mae.
    b. help Jesse with the chores because Miles left for a new job.
    c. help Mae in any way that she is able.
    d. help her parents understand the story of the Tucks.

9. Winnie asks her grandmother for some water so
    a. she can be alone in the yard with Jesse.
    b. she can water the dry flower beds.
    c. she can exchange it for some of the spring water.
    d. she can give it to the poor, thirsty toad.

10. Who appears outside the fence that evening?
    a. Mae
    b. Jesse
    c. Miles
    d. Angus

11. Winnie offers to help the Tucks out by
    a. taking Mae's place in the jailhouse.
    b. coming to their house and fixing the meals.
    c. vowing never to speak of the spring to a living soul.
    d. agreeing to destroy the spring as soon as possible.

Study Guide/Quiz Questions- *Tuck Everlasting* Multiple Choice Format Page 11

Chapter 23- Epilogue

1. Select the set of adjectives that best describes Winnie's feelings in prior to leaving to meet Jesse.
    a. restless, excited, guilty
    b. scared, excited, angry
    c. thrilled, tired, worried
    d. fearful, nervous, anxious

2. How is Miles able to help his mother?
    a. He is able to remove the window from the jailhouse so she can climb out of it.
    b. He can now bring home more income.
    c. He can teach Jesse a trade.
    d. He is able to stand up to the stranger and tell him no.

3. It finally begins to rain just as Mae climbs out of the window.
    a. true
    b. false

4. After Mae is out, Winnie
    a. hugs and kisses her.
    b. climbs in the window and poses as Mae.
    c. wishes her a safe journey.
    d. tells her she wants to come and live with her family.

5. During the night, a loud crash is caused by
    a. terrible thunder and lightning storm.
    b. the jailhouse shuddering under the weight of the rain.
    c. the gallows falling to the ground.
    d. the Tucks coming back to rescue Winnie.

6. When the constable discovers Winnie in the jail cell he calls her
    a. a criminal and an accomplice.
    b. a juvenile delinquent.
    c. an accessory to murder.
    d. a spoiled brat.

7. Were Winnie's school friends *more* or *less* attracted to her after this incident?
    a. more
    b. less

Study Guide/Quiz Questions- *Tuck Everlasting* Multiple Choice Format Page 12

8. Winnie protects the toad by
    a. taking it into her house and putting it in a cage with some grass.
    b. chasing the dog away.
    c. asking her grandmother for a stick to scare away the cat.
    d. pouring the bottled spring water over it.

9. Treegap had not changed much since the Tucks had been there.
    a. true
    b. false

10. Mae and Angus learn that
    a. Winnie died two years ago from the inscription on the tombstone.
    b. the wood burned down from an electrical storm.
    c. the spring had been bulldozed away.
    d. all of the above

11. Mae suggests that they leave Treegap for now and return in ten years.
    a. true
    b. false

12. How long had it been since Mae and Angus were in Treegap?
    a. eighty years
    b. seventy years
    c. fifty years
    d. ten years

13. What do Mae and Angus see in the road as they are leaving Treegap?
    a. a cat
    b. a toad
    c. a root from the ash tree
    d. some of the pebbles from around the spring

ANSWER KEY- MULTIPLE CHOICE STUDY/QUIZ QUESTIONS
Tuck Everlasting

Prologue- Ch. 4
1. C
2. A
3. D
4. D
5. A
6. D
7. CD
8. D
9. A
10. B
11. C
12. A

Chapters 5-8
1. B
2. A
3. C
4. D
5. B
6. C
7. B
8. D
9. A
10. B
11. C

Chapters 9-13
1. A
2. B
3. C
4. D
5. A
6. C
7. B
8. D
9. C

Chapters 14-18
1. D
2. A
3. C
4. B
5. C
6. D
7. A
8. A
9. C

Chapters 19-22
1. B
2. C
3. B
4. A
5. D
6. C
7. A
8. C
9. D
10. B
11. A

Ch. 23- Epilogue
1. A
2. A
3. A
4. B
5. C
6. A
7. A
8. D
9. B
10. D
11. B
12. B
13. B

PREREADING VOCABULARY WORKSHEETS

Vocabulary - *Tuck Everlasting*

Prologue- Chapter 4 **Part I:** Using Prior Knowledge and Contextual Clues
Below are the sentences in which the vocabulary words appear in the text. Read the sentence. Use any clues you can find in the sentence combined with your prior knowledge, and write what you think the underlined words mean on the lines provided.

1. It wandered along in curves and easy angles, swayed off and up in a pleasant *tangent* to the top of a small hill, ambled down again between fringes of bee-hung clover, and then cut sidewise across a meadow.

   _____

2-4. It widened and seemed to pause, suggesting *tranquil* *bovine* picnics, slow chewing and thoughtful contemplation of the *infinite*.

   _____

5-7. And all at once the sun was uncomfortably hot, the dust *oppressive*, and the *meager* grass along its edges somewhat ragged and *forlorn*.

   _____

8. He was still asleep, and the *melancholy* creases that folded his daytime face were smoothed and slack.

   _____

9. Tuck rolled over and made a *rueful* face at her. "What in the world could possibly happen to me?"

   _____

10. He laughed, gesturing in *self-deprecation* with long, thin fingers.

   _____

Vocabulary - *Tuck Everlasting* Prologue-Chapter 4 Continued

Part II: Determining the Meaning
Match the vocabulary words to their dictionary definitions. If there are words for which you cannot figure out the definition by contextual clues and by process of elimination, look them up in a dictionary.

   ___ 1. tangent   A. disapproval of self
   ___ 2. tranquil   B. limitless
   ___ 3. bovine   C. skimpy; sparse
   ___ 4. infinite   D. heavy; stifling
   ___ 5. oppressive   E. miserable; forsaken
   ___ 6. meager   F. calm; peaceful
   ___ 7. forlorn   G. sleepy; cowlike
   ___ 8. melancholy   H. mournful; pitiful
   ___ 9. rueful   I. departure
   ___10. self-deprecation   J. gloomy; woeful

Vocabulary - *Tuck Everlasting* Chapters 5-8

Part I: Using Prior Knowledge and Contextual Clues
Below are the sentences in which the vocabulary words appear in the text. Read the sentence. Use any clues you can find in the sentence combined with your prior knowledge, and write what you think the underlined words mean on the lines provided.

1. Still, it was *galling*, this having to admit she was afraid.

___

2. She merely told herself *consolingly*, "of course, while I'm in the wood, if I decide never to come back, well then, that will be that."

___

3. He was thin and sunburned, this wonderful boy, with a thick mop of curly brown hair, and he wore his battered trousers and loose grubby shirt with as much *self-assurance* as if they were silk and satin.

___

4. "That's good," said Winnie *irrelevantly.*

___

5. "Well, I still don't see why not," said Winnie *plaintively*. "I'm getting thirstier every minute.

___

6. Discovering him, seeing his surprise, and presented at once with choices, Winnie's mind *perversely* went blank.

___

7. She reached *distractedly* into the pocket of her skirt and took out the music box and, without thinking, twisted the winding key with trembling fingers.

___

Vocabulary - *Tuck Everlasting* Chapters 5-8 Continued

8. "We might as well enjoy it, long as we can't change it. You don't have to be such a *parson* all the time.

_____

9. Closing the gate on her oldest fears as she had closed the gate of her own fenced yard, she discovered the wings she'd always wished she had. And all at once she was *elated*.

_____

10. Her mother's voice, the feel of home, *receded* for the moment, and her thoughts turned forward.

_____

Part II: Determining the Meaning   Match the vocabulary words to their dictionary definitions.

___ 11. galling
___ 12. consolingly
___ 13. self-assurance
___ 14. irrelevantly
___ 15. plaintively
___ 16. perversely
___ 17. distractedly
___ 18. parson
___ 19. elated
___ 20. receded

A. uncontrollably
B. confidence
C. thrilled; overjoyed
D. annoying; irritating
E. sorrowfully
F. lessened; subsided
G. in bewilderment; confusedly
H. comfortingly; soothingly
I. minister; preacher
J. in a 'beside the point' manner

Vocabulary - *Tuck Everlasting* Chapters 9-13

Part I: Using Prior Knowledge and Contextual Clues
Below are the sentences in which the vocabulary words appear in the text. Read the sentence. Use any clues you can find in the sentence combined with your prior knowledge, and write what you think the underlined words mean on the lines provided.

1. Under the pitiless double assaults of her mother and grandmother, the cottage where she lived was always squeaking clean, mopped and swept and scored into limp *submission*.

2. The foster women had made a fortress out of duty. Within it, they were *indomitable*.

3. The kitchen came first, with an open cabinet where dishes were stacked in *perilous* towers without the least regard for their varying dimensions.

4. The parlor came next, where the furniture, loose and sloping with age, was set about *helter-skelter*.

5. Beyond this was a bedroom, where a vast and tipsy brass bed took up most of the space, but there was room beside it for the washstand with the lonely mirror, and opposite its foot a *cavernous* oak wardrobe from which leaped the faint smell of camphor.

6. And this was followed by another thought, far more *revolutionary*.

7. And suddenly the meal tasted *luxurious*.

Vocabulary - *Tuck Everlasting* Chapters 9-13 Continued

8. "Just the same, we got to get you home again, Winnie," said Tuck, standing up *decisively*.

_____

9. For she-yes, even she-would go out of the world *willy-nilly* someday.

_____

10. Winnie, struggling with the *anguish* of all these things, could only sit hunched and numb, the sound of the water rolling in her ears.

_____

Part II: Determining the Meaning: Match the vocabulary words to their dictionary definitions.

  ___ 21. submission   A. supreme; unconquerable
  ___ 22. indomitable   B. elegant; rich
  ___ 23. perilous   C. dangerous
  ___ 24. helter-skelter   D. with determination
  ___ 25. cavernous   E. willingly or unwillingly
  ___ 26. revolutionary   F. pain; suffering
  ___ 27. luxurious   G. rebellious; unique
  ___ 28. decisively   H. hollow and deep sounding
  ___ 29. willy-nilly   I. every which way; no pattern
  ___ 30. anguish   J. obedience; meekness

Vocabulary - *Tuck Everlasting* Chapters 14-18

Part I: Using Prior Knowledge and Contextual Clues
Below are the sentences in which the vocabulary words appear in the text. Read the sentence. Use any clues you can find in the sentence combined with your prior knowledge, and write what you think the underlined words mean on the lines provided.

1. I'm no *barbarian*, you can see that.

   _____

2. There's just no telling what *illiterates* like that might do.

   _____

3. Winnie thought about this *peril* to the frogs, and sighed saying, "It'd be nice if nothing ever had to die."

   _____

4. Your terrible *ordeal* is as good as over, isn't it?

   _____

5. "First they *roust* me out of bed in the middle of the night, after I been out since sunup looking for that child, and now I s'pose you're going to try to run me all the way, " he said sourly.

   _____

6. "Maybe you're in *cahoots* with the kidnappers, how do I know? You should of reported it right off, when you saw her get snatched."

   _____

7. Give those folks nice clean *accommodations.*

   _____

Vocabulary - *Tuck Everlasting* Chapters 14-18 Continued

8. 'Course, we got a <u>gallows</u> of our own, if we ever need it.

_____

9. "Did you get a <u>gander</u> at that suit of clothes? Oh, well, it takes all kinds, as they say."

_____

10. Winnie squinted at her fishing line and tried to picture a <u>teeming</u> world.

_____

Part II: Determining the Meaning: Match the vocabulary words to their dictionary definitions.

___ 31. barbarian   A. lodging
___ 32. illiterates   B. burden; trial
___ 33. peril   C. danger
___ 34. ordeal   D. bustling; swarming
___ 35. roust   E. savage; brute
___ 36. cahoots   F. to bring out of a state of sleep
___ 37. accommodations   G. partnership
___ 38. gallows   H. unlearned; ignorant people
___ 39. gander   I. look
___ 40. teeming   J. hanging structure

Vocabulary - *Tuck Everlasting* Chapters 19-22

Part I: Using Prior Knowledge and Contextual Clues
Below are the sentences in which the vocabulary words appear in the text. Read the sentence. Use any clues you can find in the sentence combined with your prior knowledge, and write what you think the underlined words mean on the lines provided.

1. I went to a university, I studied philosophy, *metaphysics*, even a little medicine.

_____

2. The tension in the parlor was *immense*.

_____

3. The man in the yellow suit raised his eyebrows and a nervous *petulance* came into his voice.

_____

4. The man in the yellow suit smiled a *ghastly* smile.

_____

5. Your selfishness is really quite *extraordinary*, and worse than that, you're stupid.

_____

6. Children are much more *appealing* anyway.

_____

7. "That's right," said Winnie *unflinchingly*. "They're my friends."

_____

8. His eyes were closed now, but except for that, he looked more than ever like a *marionette*, a marionette flung carelessly into a corner, arms and legs every which way midst tangled strings.

_____

Vocabulary - *Tuck Everlasting* Chapters 19-22 Continued

9. It was as if he were entranced and -yes, *envious*- like a starving man looking through a window at a banquet.

_____

10. There was a pause, and the murmur of other voices; then a match striking, the *acrid* smell of fresh cigar smoke.

_____

Part II: Determining the Meaning: Match the vocabulary words to their dictionary definitions.

___ 41. metaphysics   A. bitter; harsh
___ 42. immense   B. amazing; remarkable
___ 43. petulance   C. unafraid; unhesitantly
___ 44. ghastly   D. pleasing; charming
___ 45. extraordinary   E. crossness; irritability
___ 46. appealing   F. puppet
___ 47. unflinchingly   G. giant; huge
___ 48. marionette   H. jealous; resentful
___ 49. envious   I. branch of science
___ 50. acrid   J. dreadful; horrible

Vocabulary - *Tuck Everlasting* Chapters 23- Epilogue

Part I: Using Prior Knowledge and Contextual Clues
Below are the sentences in which the vocabulary words appear in the text. Read the sentence. Use any clues you can find in the sentence combined with your prior knowledge, and write what you think the underlined words mean on the lines provided.

1., 2. The sun was a *ponderous* circle without edges, a roar without a sound, a blazing glare so thorough and *remorseless* that even in the Fosters' parlor, with curtains drawn, it seemed an actual presence.

_____

3. It was totally unlike them, this lapse from *gentility*, and it made them much more interesting.

_____

4. "It's going to rain, I think," she told the *prostrate* group in the parlor, and the news was received with little moans of gratitude.

_____

5. Her hips were free-now, look out!- here she came, her skirts tearing on the rough edges of the boards, arms *flailing*- and they were all in a heap on the ground.

_____

6. Another crash of thunder muffled Jesse's bursting *exultant* laugh. Mae was free.

_____

7. As she watched, one of these detached itself into a sudden breeze and sailed *sedately* off, while others leaned from the pod as if to observe its departure.

_____

8. A feeling of *revulsion* swept through her.

_____

Vocabulary - *Tuck Everlasting* Chapters 23- Epilogue Continued

9. This of all things her family understood, and afterward they drew together *staunchly* around her.

_____

10. She was ...an *accomplice*. She had helped a murderer escape.

_____

Part II: Determining the Meaning: Match the vocabulary words to their dictionary definitions.

___ 51. ponderous   A. elegance; grace
___ 52. remorseless   B. ecstatic; thrilled
___ 53. gentility   C. partner; accessory
___ 54. prostrate   D. dull; dreary
___ 55. flailing   E. thrashing
___ 56. exultant   F. loyally; faithfully
___ 57. sedately   G. calmly
___ 58. revulsion   H. worn out; exhausted
___ 59. staunchly   I. disgust; distaste
___ 60. accomplice   J. without regret

ANSWER KEY - VOCABULARY
Tuck Everlasting

Prologue-Chapter 4
1. I
2. F
3. G
4. B
5. D
6. C
7. E
8. J
9. H
10. A

Chapters 5-8
11. D
12. H
13. B
14. J
15. E
16. A
17. G
18. I
19. C
20. F

Chapters 9-13
21. J
22. A
23. C
24. I
25. H
26. G
27. B
28. D
29. E
30. F

Chapters 14-18
31. E
32. H
33. C
34. B
35. F
36. G
37. A
38. J
39. I
40. D

Chapters 19-22
41. I
42. G
43. E
44. J
45. B
46. D
47. C
48. F
49. H
50. A

Chapters 23-Epilogue
51. D
52. J
53. A
54. H
55. E
56. B
57. G
58. I
59. F
60. C

DAILY LESSONS

LESSON ONE

Objectives
    1. To introduce the *Tuck Everlasting* unit
    2. To introduce the theme of everlasting life
    3. To distribute books and other related materials
    4. To model effective oral reading skills by reading the prologue and chapter 1 aloud to the class
    5. To have students identify the setting and point of view

Activity #1

    Begin lesson by asking students the advantages and disadvantages of being ten or eleven years old. Continue by discussing advantages and disadvantages of various other ages by small groups (i. e each group discuss a different age). Focus on the most desirable age reached by class consensus. Ask students how they would feel if they could live forever and what makes them feel that way.

TRANSITION: Explain to students that *Tuck Everlasting*, the book they are about to read, is a fantasy. Allow students to share their concept of what comprises a fantasy and ask them to share other fantasies they have read and what makes them a fantasy. Then explain that something fantastic has happened to four of the characters in our novel, they have been the same age for eighty-seven years, without changing one bit. They have everlasting life!

Activity #2

    Distribute the materials students will use in this unit. Explain in detail how students are to use these materials.

    Study Guides Students should preview the study guide questions before each reading assignment to get a feeling for what events and ideas are important in that section. After reading the section, students will (as a class or individually) answer the questions to review the important events and ideas from that section of the book. Students should keep the study guides as study materials for the unit test.

    Vocabulary Prior to reading a reading assignment, students will do vocabulary work related to the section of the book they are about to read. Following the completion of the reading of the book, there will be a vocabulary review of all the words used in the vocabulary assignments. Students should keep their vocabulary work as study materials for the unit test.

<u>Reading Assignment Sheet</u>   You need to fill in the reading assignment sheet to let students know when their reading has to be completed. You can either write the assignment sheet on a side blackboard or bulletinboard and leave it there for students to see each day, or you can "ditto" copies for each student to have. In either case, you should advise students to become very familiar with the reading assignments so they know what is expected of them.

<u>Extra Activities Center</u>   The Unit Resource portion of this unit contains suggestions for a library of related books and articles in your classroom as well as crossword and word search puzzles. Make an extra activities center in your room where you will keep these materials for students to use. (Bring the books and articles in from the library and keep several copies of the puzzles on hand.) Explain to students that these materials are available for students to use when they finish reading assignments or other class work early.

<u>Nonfiction Assignment Sheet</u>   Explain to students that they each are to read at least one non-fiction piece from the in-class library at some time during the unit. Students will fill out a nonfiction assignment sheet after completing the reading to help you (the teacher evaluate their reading experiences and to help the students think about and evaluate their own reading experiences.

<u>Books</u>   Each school has its own rules and regulations regarding student use of school books. Advise students of the procedures that are normal for your school.

<u>Activity #2</u>

Give the class time to examine the book and read the cover summary. Point out the short chapters and the prologue and epilogue as well as the primary color of the book cover.

<u>Activity #3</u>

Read the prologue and chapter 1 aloud to the class stopping to help them identify point of view (third person) and setting.

<u>Activity #4</u>

Assign the prereading vocabulary, the study guide preview, and the reading for the first set of pages (prologue-chapter 4) to be done by Lesson Two. If time, begin in class.

LESSON TWO

Objectives
1. To review the main events and ideas from Prologue-chapter 4
2. To preview the study questions for chapters 5-8
3. To familiarize students with the vocabulary in chapters 5-8
4. To review vocabulary from Prologue-chapter 4

Activity #1
Discuss the answers to the study questions for prologue-chapter 4 in detail. Write the answers on the board or overhead transparency so students can have the correct answers for study purposes. Note: It is a good practice in public speaking and leadership skills for individual students to take charge of leading the discussions of the study questions. Perhaps a different student could go to the front of the class and lead the discussion each day that the study questions are discussed during this unit. Of course, the teacher should guide the discussion when appropriate and be sure to fill in any gaps the students leave.

Activity #2
As a whole class, look over study guide questions for chapters 5-8 having students read them aloud individually. Do the same for the prereading vocabulary sentences and matching section.

Activity #3
Pair students up with a partner. Using their vocabulary sheets from the first section of reading, have one of the pair give the other a synonym for one of the vocabulary words. The other partner must look only at the sentences and try to say the correct vocabulary word in response. Continue until all 10 words have been covered. If doing well with that, have them give their partner an antonym for the vocabulary word to see if they can come up with the right word.

LESSON THREE

Objectives
1. To read chapters 5-8
2. To give students practice reading orally
3. To evaluate students' oral reading

Activity
Have students read chapters 5-8 orally in class. You probably know the best way to get readers within your class; pick students at random, ask for volunteers, have students who have just read select another student, assign numbers to students and spin a spinner, whatever works best for you. Complete the oral reading evaluation form that follows this lesson after listening to your students read.

ORAL READING EVALUATION - *Tuck Everlasting*

Name _____ Class____ Date _____

SKILL	EXCELLENT	GOOD	AVERAGE	FAIR	POOR
Fluency	5	4	3	2	1
Clarity	5	4	3	2	1
Audibility	5	4	3	2	1
Pronunciation	5	4	3	2	1
_____	5	4	3	2	1
_____	5	4	3	2	1

Total _____   Grade _____

Comments:

LESSON FOUR

Objectives
1. To review the main events and ideas from chapters 5-8
2. To review the vocabulary from Prologue-chapter 8
3. To give students the opportunity to practice writing to express personal ideas

Activity #1

Use the multiple choice format of the study guide questions for chapters 5-8 as a quiz to check that students have done the required reading and to review the main ideas of chapters 5-8. Exchange papers for checking. Discuss answers and make sure students take notes for studying purposes.

Activity #2

Have students look over the vocabulary work for Prologue-chapter 8 for about 10 minutes. Use the matching section of the vocabulary pages as a springboard for a game similar to concentration. Divide students into groups of four or five. Have students quickly copy the vocabulary words (divide the task into sections to expedite) and their clues on separate index cards. Turn them all over. Have students in their small groups take turns flipping over two of the cards. If they are a match, i.e. a vocabulary word matches with its meaning, they keep the pair and get another turn. Students may look at the vocabulary words in their sentences for contextual clues. Continue play until all cards are matched into sets.

Activity #3

Distribute Writing Assignment #1 and discuss the directions in detail. Allow remaining class time for students to work on the assignment. Inform them this paper will be due by Lesson Six so you will have time to evaluate them before their writing conference to be held during Lesson Nine

WRITING ASSIGNMENT #1 - *Tuck Everlasting*

PROMPT

This entire story revolves around the secret of the magic spring. As you are now aware, the Tucks came across this place purely by coincidence. They were thirsty and drank from the spring unknowingly. If they would have known the spring's power, do you think they still would have drunk it?

Your assignment is to state your position on drinking from the spring. Would you personally, if you had the opportunity, drink from the magical water and gain eternal life? Or would you select to live out a normal life cycle like the rest of us mortals?

PREWRITING

A good way to start is to think about what it would be like to remain the same age forever. What would be the advantages, the disadvantages? How would you spend your time? How would you relate to your friends and family who would continue to age when you wouldn't. Do the positive points outweigh the negative ones in your mind? Make notes about these and any other ideas you may have concerning this topic.

DRAFTING

You should begin your paper with an introductory paragraph giving your reader some background information on this novel's plot and your possible opportunity. Include the personal decision you have made.

The body of your composition should contain all the reasons you chose the decision you made. Use your notes about the good and bad points to help you get started. This is where you need to include your feelings and attitudes about the decision you made and why you made it.

Write a final paragraph in which you conclude how this decision would affect your life and how you would handle it.

PROMPT

When you finish the rough draft of your paper, ask a student who sits near you to read it. After reading your rough draft, he/she should tell you what he/she liked best about your work, which parts were difficult to understand, and ways in which your work could be improved. Reread your paper considering your critic's comments, and make the corrections you think are necessary.

PROOFREADING

Do a final proofreading of your paper double-checking your grammar, spelling, organization, and the clarity of your ideas.

LESSON FIVE

Objectives
    1. To familiarize students with vocabulary from chapters 9-13
    2. To preview study questions for chapters 9-13
    3. To give students the opportunity to fulfill their nonfiction reading assignment

Activity #1
    Have students pair up to do prereading vocabulary work from chapters 9-13 and to preview study questions for chapters 9-13.

Activity #2
    Assign reading of these chapters to be completed by the next class session. Students may begin this assignment if they have completed their nonfiction reading assignment.

Activity #3
    Allow students who have not completed their nonfiction reading form, to go to the library at this time to find an appropriate selection. Perhaps you could hold class in the library for this Lesson.

LESSON SIX

Objectives
    1. To review main events and ideas in chapters 9-13
    2. To do the prereading vocabulary work for chapters 14-18
    3. To preview study guide questions for chapters 14-18

Activity #1
    Use the multiple choice study guide questions for chapters 9-13 as a quiz to test students reading of assigned text and as a review of the main ideas. Exchange papers to check. Discuss answers to insure understanding. Encourage note taking for their later study use.

Activity #2
    Have students spend about 10 minutes completing the prereading vocabulary page for chapters 14-18. After they have done that, pair them up. Have one member of each pair "act" out one of the words, while the other one tries to guess the word. Do this until all of the vocabulary words have been covered at least once. This is similar to the game Charades. If extra time, include vocabulary from earlier chapters as a review.

Activity #3
    Have students preview study guide questions independently for chapters 14-18 in the remaining class time.

NONFICTION READING ASSIGNMENT SHEET - *Tuck Everlasting*
(To be completed after reading the required nonfiction article)

Name _____ Date _____

Title of Nonfiction Read _____

Written By _____ Publication Date _____

I. Factual Summary: Write a short summary of the piece you read.

II. Vocabulary
 1. With which vocabulary words in the piece did you encounter some degree of difficulty?

 2. How did you resolve your lack of understanding with these words?

III. Interpretation: What was the main point the author wanted you to get from reading his work?

IV. Criticism
 1. With which points of the piece did you agree or find easy to accept? Why?

 2. With which points of the piece did you disagree or find difficult to believe? Why?

V. Personal Response: What do you think about this piece? OR How does this piece influence your ideas?

LESSON SEVEN

Objectives
1. To review the main ideas of chapters 14-18
2. To do the prereading vocabulary work for chapters 19-22
3. To preview the study questions for chapters 19-22
4. To expose figurative language to students

Activity #1

Hand out four little slips of paper or mini cards to each student that have the letters A,B,C, or D on them. A good idea is to use different color cards for each letter. Use the multiple choice study guide questions and answers on Chapters 14-18 for an oral review. Read the question (and/ or show it on the overhead). Then give students the four possible answers, labeling them A, B, C, or D (or show on overhead again). Students respond by holding up the card with what they think is the correct answer. This is one variety of Every Student Response. Remind students not to look at what others are holding up, but to simply display the card of their choice. This is a quick indicator of students' comprehension. You can make it somewhat different by requiring complete silence and having them read the questions silently from the overhead, or make it more mysterious (fun?) by blindfolding everyone and have them hold up a certain number of fingers per answer instead of using the cards.

Activity #2

Have students pair up and do the prereading work together for chapters 19-22

Activity #3

Give students remaining time to review chapters 19-22 study guide questions. Inform them that the completion of the reading of these chapters is due by class Lesson Nine.

Activity #4

Within the last 5-8 minutes of class, turn the class's attention to your reading of the following examples of figurative language from their recent reading (just ask them to listen):

- the cushions were remarkably lumpy and smelled like old newspapers
- the wide world shrank and her oldest fears rolled freely in her consciousness
- Proud as peacocks, all of 'em
- the lily pads lay like upturned palms on the surface
- Jesse was like water: thin and quick
- a dragonfly, a brilliant blue jewel darted up
- rainbow-colored scales, and an eye like a marble

Inquire if they see any similarities in these passages, or have any idea what these are examples of? Encourage them to do some research tonight if no one comes up with "figures of speech" (personification, etc.) or "figurative language". Tell them that in the next class session they will become very familiar with these and many more passages like them from their novel.

LESSON EIGHT

Objectives
    1. To introduce simile, personification, and metaphor as figures of speech
    2. To distinguish between three different types of figurative language
    3. To have students locate figurative language in the text
    4. To create original figures of speech
    5. To illustrate figurative language

Activity #1

Review any of the previous introduction that was successful. If any students identified the passages correctly, continue allowing them to explain. If not, once again read some examples from the text and determine what makes them figurative language. Make three columns on the chalkboard labeling each one separately: simile, metaphor, and personification. Spend some time here instructing about these three forms of figurative language. Perhaps you could cite some examples from familiar songs. Ask why they think any author or lyricist would use them? Do they use them? Why? In what way does using them enhance speaking or writing or the understanding of each of these. As a whole group, have students give you examples they can think of and then have them locate a few in any part of the text they have read. Allow them to come to the board and write these under the correct heading. When you are satisfied with their ability to recognize them go to the next activity.

Activity #2

Divide the class into small groups of three or four. Have each group assign a recorder. Give them a couple of sheets of paper. Ask each group to locate as many of these figures of speech as they can from the text. They may be more successful in the portion they already have read, but it isn't necessary to limit them. Giving them a time constraint is an option. It could be a race, you are the judge. Offer a special incentive for the group that can most quickly find the figurative language-rich beginning chapter page that has two similes, three personifications, and one metaphor (page 91, chapter 8). You may want to rule out using the ones that are posted on the board. It's up to you. There are a wealth of them present in the text, they'll find plenty. Wrap this activity up by having the group with the **most** read their list aloud. Decide as a whole group if indeed each one is correct. Have all groups check off the ones that are read that they also found. Allow every group to read any that have not yet been mentioned. You could give small treats for first, second, third place, etc.

Activity #3
Have students create one example of each type. They could be individual sentences or you could require them to write a short paragraph using all three. Base this on the ability level of your students and/or time. Create one together as a model. If time, have them illustrate it with original art work or magazine pictures. Save finished products for display. They could do this part as homework.

NOTE: The following figurative language test is optional. You may want to use it right after instruction, later in unit, or not at all. You may choose to use it only as a resource for this lesson. It contains examples from the entire book.

FIGURATIVE LANGUAGE TEST - *Tuck Everlasting*

I. Read the following examples of figurative language. Label each one separately with either an **S** for simile, **P** for personification, or an **M** for metaphor. **BONUS**: Circle the **3** that are both an S and a P. *Super Sleuth Award*: Locate **one** that contains all three.

1. The first week of August hangs at the very top of summer, the top of the live-long year, like the highest seat of a Ferris wheel when it pauses in its turning. _____
2. And that would have been a disaster so immense that this weary old earth, owned or not to its fiery core, would have trembled on its axis like a bottle on a pin._____
3. Mae sat there frowning, a great potato of a woman with a round, sensible face and calm brown eyes._____
4. But at the same time he had a kind of grace, like a well-handled marionette. _____
5. The last stains had melted away, and the twilight died too, as he stood there, though its remnants clung reluctantly to everything that was pale in color-pebbles, the dusty road, the figure of the man himself- turning them blue and blurry. _____
6. The sun was just opening its own eye on the eastern horizon._____
7. He wore his battered trousers and loose, grubby shirt with as much self-assurance as if they were silk and satin._____
8. I'm about dry as dust._____
9. Her backbone felt like a pipe full of cold running water_____
10. It was like a ribbon tying her to familiar things._____
11. They gathered around her like children at their mother's knee.____
12. The sweet earth opened out its wide four corners to her like the petals of a flower ready to be picked, and it shimmered with light and possibility till she was dizzy with it._____
13. Queen Anne's lace lay dusty on the surface of the meadows like foam on a painted sea._____
14. Winnie saw an expression there that made her feel like an unexpected present, wrapped in pretty paper and tied with ribbons._____
15. For, on the old beamed ceiling of the parlor, streaks of light swam and danced and wavered like a bright mirage, reflected through the windows from the sunlit surface of the pond._____
16. The sky was a ragged blaze of red and pink and orange, and its double trembled on the surface of the pond like color spilled from a paintbox. _____
17. The sun was dropping fast now, a soft red sliding egg yolk, and already to the east there was a darkening to purple._____
18. In the fading light, the trees along the banks were slowly losing their dimensions, flattening into silhouettes clipped from black paper and pasted to the paling sky._____
19. Just go out, like the flame of a candle, and no use protesting. _____
20. The people would have turned into nothing but rocks by the side of the road._____

II. List one example of your own for each type of figurative language. They can be original or from your favorite songs.

ANSWER KEY FIGURATIVE LANGUAGE TEST - *Tuck Everlasting*

I.
1. P, S
2. S
3. M
4. S
5. P
6. P
7. P
8. S
9. S
10. S
11. S
12. P, S
13. S
14. S
15. P, S
16. M, P, S
17. M
18. M
19. S
20. M

II. Answers will vary.

LESSON NINE

Objectives
1. To evaluate students' writing
2. To give students an opportunity to produce an error-free paper and to apply the teacher's suggestions
3. To complete the reading of chapters 19-22

Activity #1

Allow students to read chapters 19-22 silently at their desks. If they finish this, have them work on illustrating some of their favorite figurative language from the novel.

Activity #2

Call students to your desk (or some other private area) to discuss their papers from Writing Assignment 1. Use the following Writing Evaluation Form to help structure your conference.

Activity #3

After the writing conference, allow students to revise their papers using your suggestions and corrections. Give them about three days from the date they receive their papers to complete the revision. I suggest grading the revisions on an A-C-E scale (all revisions well-done, some revisions made, few or no revisions made). This will speed your grading time and still give some credit for the students' efforts. Give students a date when revisions are due.

WRITING EVALUATION FORM - *Tuck Everlasting*

Name _____ Date _____

Writing Assignment #1 for the *Tuck Everlasting* unit   Grade _____

Circle One For Each Item:

Description (paragraph 1)	excellent	good	fair	poor
Plans (body paragraphs)	excellent	workable	fair	not realistic
Conclusion	excellent	good	fair	poor
Grammar:	excellent	good	fair	poor (errors noted)
Spelling:	excellent	good	fair	poor (errors noted)
Punctuation:	excellent	good	fair	poor (errors noted)
Legibility:	excellent	good	fair	poor

Strengths:

Weaknesses:

Comments/Suggestions:

LESSON TEN

Objectives
    1. To review the main ideas of chapters 19-22
    2. To give students the opportunity to write to inform by developing and organizing facts to convey information

Activity #1

As a whole class go over the answers to the study guide questions as done previously in Lesson Two.

Activity #2

Distribute Writing Assignment #2 and discuss the directions in detail. Give students the remainder of class time to work on this assignment. Provide them with a due date.

LESSON ELEVEN

Objectives
    1. To preview the study guide questions for chapters 23- Epilogue
    2. To preview the prereading vocabulary work for chapters 23- Epilogue
    3. To work on Writing Assignment #2

Activity #1

Have students spend approximately 10 minutes completing the prereading vocabulary work independently. Pass out plain paper for drawing, or use individual easels or slates. Have one of the partners sketch their impression of one of the vocabulary words within a limited amount of time. The other one is to guess which vocabulary word he/she is trying to picture. When the correct word has been chosen, play turns to the other partner. Continue play until all vocabulary has been covered for chapters 23-Epilogue. This is similar to the game Pictionary. It could also be done in small groups. Once again, if time, incorporate vocabulary from earlier chapters.

Activity #2

Individually, have students look over the study guide questions for chapter 23- Epilogue.

Activity #3

Allow students remaining class time to work on their Advertisements providing them with materials they may need.

WRITING ASSIGNMENT #2 - *Tuck Everlasting*

PROMPT

After reading chapters 19-22 of *Tuck Everlasting,* you know that the man in the yellow suit planned to sell the magical spring water to make a profit for himself. He even offered the Tucks the position of helping him advertise the powers of the water.

Your assignment is to create and design an advertisement that the man in the yellow suit may have used to sell the spring water. Your advertisement should carry all the usual information that an advertisement would contain such as : clarity, appeal, lettering, graphics, colorful language, product description, testimonials, etc. Your ad must fit on an 8 1/2" X 11" sheet of paper. Be as creative as you like, but remember your ad must contain the information requested above and remember that you are striving for an effective advertisement.

PREWRITING

The first thing you need to do is to jot down ideas you have about what would be the best selling point or points of your product; what would be the best approach to take to sell the most? How can you get these ideas across in a minimal amount of space.

Put down all of your thoughts, and then go back and sort through them. Combine ideas that are essentially the same. Organize your thoughts into the categories you want to present. From there you can begin to design your ad.

DRAFTING

You need to make a few basic decisions: Are you going to have any graphics (drawings) in your ad? Will you have a background? What will be the attention-getter in your ad? How can you make all of your most important information fit on one page? How will you lay-out or design your ad? How will it look on the page? What type of lettering will you use? Once you have decided these things, you can put pencil to paper and make a rough draft of your ad.

PROMPT

After you have finished a rough draft of your ad, revise it yourself until you are happy with your work. Then, ask a student who sits near you to tell you what he/she likes best about your work, and what things he/she thinks can be improved. Take another look at your ad keeping in mind your critic's suggestions, and make the revisions you feel are necessary.

PROOFREADING

Do a final proofreading of your paper double-checking your grammar, spelling, organization, and the clarity of your ideas.

LESSON TWELVE

Objectives
1. To read the ending of the novel aloud in class together
2. To recognize a character as an antagonist or protagonist

Activity #1

Read the final chapters aloud together using techniques to get class to read aloud listed in Lesson Three, if needed. Examine how the ending was similar or different from what they expected. Elicit students' response concerning Winnie's final actions: taking Mae's place in the jailhouse and pouring the water over the toad. Were these actions predictable?

Activity #2

Extend Activity #1 by introducing antagonist and protagonist as types of literary characters. Explain that the author generally pits the main character/s against some other person or group of persons. This conflict can also be against environment, or against some element of his own nature. The central character in the conflict is the *protagonist*; the forces set against him, whether persons, or otherwise are the *antagonist*. Draw the following chart on the board to plot information from this novel.

CONFLICT	PROTAGONIST	ANTAGONIST

LESSON THIRTEEN

Objectives
    1. To review the main ideas and events from chapters 23-Epilogue
    2. To give students the opportunity to write to persuade

Activity #1
    Have students pair up and quiz each other's comprehension using the study guide questions or the multiple choice format.

Activity #2
    Distribute Writing Assignment #3 and discuss the directions in detail. Give students the remainder of class time to work on this assignment. Provide them with a due date.

WRITING ASSIGNMENT #3 - *Tuck Everlasting*

PROMPT

Now that you have completed reading *Tuck Everlasting*, you know that Mae Tuck was to be hanged for killing the man in the yellow suit. Mae, a seemingly nonviolent person, chose violence to prevent the stranger from using Winnie in his sinister plot to sell the spring water. In this novel, there was no mention of a trial, just that "it was an open-and-shut case" since the constable was an eyewitness. In reconsidering this action, one could ask if, indeed, Mae made the correct decision. If the man in the yellow suit had been taken to trial, perhaps he would have been found guilty of extortion or worse and been sentenced to jail.

In this writing assignment, we're putting Mae on trial for murdering the stranger. You are to become either the attorney for Mae's defense or the prosecuting attorney. Your assignment is to write your closing arguments to the jury. (Closing arguments are a lawyer's final summary of his case and his best efforts at persuading the jury to his side.)

PREWRITING

To begin, decide which side you want to take--Mae's defense or the prosecution. On a piece of paper, jot down the main points, the facts which will support your case. Decide which points are your strongest and which of the arguments you will make are weaker. Organize your points from weakest to strongest and jot down anything you can think of which will support or explain your points.

DRAFTING

Begin with an introductory paragraph in which you introduce the jury to your side of the case. Follow that with one paragraph for each of the main points you have to support your case. Fill in each paragraph with examples and facts which support your main point. Then, write a paragraph in which you make your final closing statements.

PROMPT

When you finish your rough draft, ask a student who sits near you to read it. After reading your rough draft, he/she should tell you what he/she liked best about your work, which parts were difficult to understand, and ways in which your work could be improved. Reread your paper considering your critic's comments and make the corrections you think are necessary.

PROOFREADING

Do a final proofreading of your paper double-checking your grammar, spelling, organization, and the clarity of your ideas.

LESSONS FOURTEEN AND FIFTEEN

Objectives
1. To discuss the ideas and themes from *Tuck Everlasting* in greater detail
2. To have students exercise their interpretive and critical thinking skills
3. To try to relate some of the ideas in *Tuck Everlasting* to the students' lives

Activity #1

Choose the questions from the Extra Discussion Questions/Writing Assignments which seem most appropriate for your students. A class discussion of these questions is most effective if students have been given the opportunity to formulate answers to the questions prior to the discussion. To this end, you may either have all the students formulate answers to all the questions, divide your class into groups and assign one or more questions to each group, or you could assign one question to each student in your class. The option you choose will make a difference in the amount of class time needed for this activity.

Activity #2

After students have had ample time to formulate answers to the questions, begin your class discussion of the questions and the ideas presented by the questions. Be sure students take notes during the discussion so they have information to study for the unit test.

EXTRA DISCUSSION QUESTIONS/WRITING ASSIGNMENTS
Tuck Everlasting

Interpretive

1. From what point of view is this story told? How would the story change if told from only one character's point of view?

2. Identify the setting. How does it influence the plot of this novel?

3. Are the characters in *Tuck Everlasting* stereotypes (characters who conform to a common type; reflect prejudices about each other)? If so, explain why an author would include stereotypes in a book.

4. What are the main conflicts in the story, and how are they resolved?

5. What is foreshadowing? Give examples of foreshadowing used in *Tuck Everlasting*.

6. Why do you think the toad was introduced to the story?

7. Complete a character sketch for Winnie.

8. Formulate an accurate time line for the novel beginning with the August morning Mae goes to meet her sons through when the Tucks return in the Epilogue.

9. Explain the role of each of these characters: the man in the yellow suit, Mae, Miles, Jesse, Angus, the constable, and Winnie's parents.

10. Define climax. Next, summarize the main events leading up to **it** and the remaining events after **it** that create the resolution.

11. Locate examples of the dialect some of the characters use. Did its use influence your opinion of these characters? Why do some speak that way, while others do not?

Critical

12. Explain the significance of the title "*Tuck Everlasting*".

13. How had Winnie developed her sense of *rightness* when she had so few experiences?

14. Were the Tucks "good" people? Why or why not?

15. Why was the first week in the month of August chosen to be of such importance in this novel?

Tuck Everlasting Extra Discussion Questions page 2

16. Do you agree with the author's statement, "nothing seems interesting when it belongs to you"?

17. For what reason do you think Natalie Babbitt would write a fantasy about everlasting life for young readers?

18. Why does the concept of the "wheel" keep reappearing throughout the book?

19. Why does Winnie pour the everlasting water over the toad instead of drinking it herself?

20. Describe Natalie Babbitt's writing style, including her use of figurative language. How does it shape the story?

21. What did you learn from the story of *Tuck Everlasting?*

22. Angus explains his view on the cycle of life to Winnie when they are in the rowboat. Is his information accurate?

23. What do you think the stranger's "yellow" suit represented? His black hat? Where else do you see any of these colors?

24. Were you surprised at the courage young ten-year-old Winnie showed in the face of kidnaping and helping Mae escape from jail? Why or why not? How would you have handled those situations?

25. Why was the small town called Treegap?

26. Why does the rain finally start after Mae is out of the jailhouse?

27. What significance can be attached to the crashing gallows during the night Winnie is in the jailhouse posing as Mae?

Critical/ Personal Response

28. Both Winnie and Miles wanted to do something important and make a difference in the world. Did they? Support your opinion. What could you do at your age to make a difference?

29. Have you read any other books written by Natalie Babbitt? How do they compare to *Tuck Everlasting*? Which one is your favorite? Why?

Tuck Everlasting Extra Discussion Questions page 3

30. Winnie lies to the constable and tells him she willingly came with the Tucks; that they did not kidnap her. Why does she say that? Have you ever been in a similar position?

31. Should Winnie have saved the bottle of spring water Jesse gave her and drank it later? Why or why not? What would you have done?

32. Did Mae do the right thing when she hit the stranger in the skull with the rifle? Why or why not? What else could have been done? Could it have been handled without violence?

33. Compare and contrast the main character's parents to yours. Do you feel your parents are overprotective like Winnie's? Why or why not?

34. Evaluate the stranger's plan for the spring. Had you discovered this fantastic secret, would your plan for it be similar or different? Share.

35. Why wasn't Winnie allowed to leave her fenced yard? How did that make her feel? Can you relate to how Winnie felt? Explain.

36. Why did Winnie decide to keep the secret of the spring? What would you have done? Is it always good to keep a secret? When wouldn't it be a good thing?

Personal Response
37. On page 7 the author raises the question of land ownership. Does it go all the way to the center of the earth?

38. Have you ever experienced a change of status among your peers like Winnie did due to her experience? What happened to you?

39. What is the value of believing in yourself and your sense of "rightness" when it may not appear *right* to those around you? Can you share a time you had to do what you thought was right, like Winnie, despite others' differing opinion?

40. Were you surprised at the courage young ten-year-old Winnie showed in the face of her kidnaping and helping Mae escape from jail? How would you have handled those situations?

41. As Winnie waits to meet Jesse the night of the planned escape, she is feeling guilty because she is purposely choosing to disobey her parents. Did you ever feel like that?

Tuck Everlasting Extra Discussion Questions page 4

42. Are you or anyone you know an only child like Winnie? What are the advantages? Disadvantages?

43. Explain what these lines from an old poem on page 123 mean to you, "Stone walls do not a prison make, Nor iron bars a cage." Why do you think Winnie thought of them when she did?

44. Mae's music box played a major role in this story. Do you or someone you know have a music box? How does its music affect you?

45. Winnie changes her mind about the Tucks and the man in the yellow suit as the story develops. Have you ever had a first impression about someone that was totally wrong?

Quotations

1. "The boys'll be home tomorrow."

2. "Why should you have to be cooped up in a cage, too? It'd be better if I could be like you, out in the open and making up my own mind. Do you know they hardly ever let me out of this yard all by myself? I'll never be able to do anything important if I stay in here like this. I expect I better run away."

3. "How delightful to see you looking so fit."

4. "I'm looking for someone. A family."

5. "Did you hear that Winifred? That's it! That's the elf music I told you about. Why, it's been ages since I heard it last. And this is the first time you've ever heard it, isn't it? Wait till we tell your father."

6. " I didn't mean to watch you, I didn't know anyone would be here."

7. "Is that good to drink? I'm thirsty."

8. "Believe me, Winnie Foster, it would be terrible for you if you drank any of this water. Just terrible. I can't let you."

9. "Well, boys, here it is. The worst is happening at last."

Tuck Everlasting Extra Discussion Questions page 5

10. "Dear Lord, don't cry! Please don't cry, child! We're not bad people, truly we're not. We had to bring you away-you'll see why in a minute- and we'll take you back just as soon as we can. Tomorrow. I promise."

11. "Yes, don't leave that out. We all had a drink, except for the cat."

12. "Pa thinks it's something left over from-well, from some other plan for the way the world should be, some plan that didn't work out too good. And so everything was changed. Except that the spring was passed over, somehow or other. Maybe he's right. I don't know."

13. "It feels so fine to tell somebody! Just think Winnie Foster, you're the only person in the world, besides us, who knows about it!"

14. "There's just no words to tell you how happy I am to see you. It's the finest thing that's happened in....-oh- at least eighty years. "

15. "Tuck and me, we got each other, and that's a lot. The boys, now, they go their separate ways. They're some different, don't always get on too good. But they come home whenever the spirit moves, and every ten year, first week of August, they meet at the spring and come home together so's we can be a family again for a little while."

16. "We got to get you home just as fast as we can. I got a feeling this whole thing is going to come apart like wet bread. But first we got to talk, and the pond's the best place. The pond's got the answers. Come along, child. Let's go out on the water."

17. "Life. Moving, growing changing, never the same two minutes together. This water, you look out at it every minute, and it looks the same, but it ain't. All night long it's been moving, coming in through the stream back there to the west, slipping out through the stream down east here, always quiet, always new, moving on. You can't hardly see the current, can you? And sometimes the wind makes it look like it's going the other way. But it's always there, the water's always moving on, and someday, after a long while, it comes to the ocean."

18. "It's a wheel, Winnie. Everything's a wheel, turning and turning, never stopping. Dying's part of the wheel, right there next to being born. You can't pick out the pieces you like and leave the rest. Being part of the whole thing, that's the blessing."

Tuck Everlasting Extra Discussion Questions page 6

19. "Can you picture what that means? Forever? The wheel would keep on going round, the water rolling by to the ocean, but the people would've turned into nothing but rocks by the side of the road. 'Cause they wouldn't know till after, and then it'd be too late. Do you see now child?"

20. "How'd it be if you was to wait till you're seventeen, same as me- heck that's only six years off- and then you could go and drink some, and then you could go away with me! We could get married, even."

21. "Now, I don't have to spell things out for people like yourselves. Some types one comes across can't seem to cut their way through any problem, and that does make things difficult. But you, I don't have to explain the situation to you. I've got what you want, and you've got what I want. Of course, you might find that child without me, but...you might not find her in time. So: I want the wood and you want the child. It's a trade. A simple, clear-cut trade."

22. "Maybe you're in cahoots with the kidnappers, how do I know? You should of reported it right off, when you saw her get snatched."

23. "You're kind of a close-lipped feller, ain't you?'"

24. "The way I see it, it's no good hiding yourself away, like Pa and lots of other people. And it's no good just thinking of your own pleasure, either. People got to do something useful if they're going to take up space in the world."

25. "People got to be meat-eaters sometimes, though. It's the natural way. And that means killing things."

26. "Good morning, Mrs. Tuck. It is Mrs. Tuck, isn't it? May I come in?"

27. "Hear me out. As I've told you, I was fascinated by my grandmother's stories. People who never grew older! It was fantastic. It took possession of me. I decided to devote my life to finding out if it could be true, and if so, how and why."

28. "Like all magnificent things, it's very simple. The wood- and the spring- belong to me now. I have the paper here, all signed and legal to prove it. I'm going to sell the water, you see."

29. "Freaks. You want us to be freaks. In a patent-medicine show."

Tuck Everlasting Extra Discussion Questions page 7

30. "I can't think why you're so upset. Did you really believe you could keep that water for yourselves? Your selfishness is really quite extraordinary and worse than that, you're stupid. You could have done what I'm about to do, long ago. Now it's too late. Once Winifred drinks some of the water, she'll do just as well for my demonstrations. Even better. Children are much more appealing anyway."

31. "Not Winnie! You ain't going to do a thing like that to Winnie. And you ain't going to give out the secret."

32. "They'd all come running like pigs to slop."

33. "Yep, she got him a good one, all right. He never even come to. So it's an open-and-shut case, since I seen her do it. Eyewitness. No question about it. They'll hang her for sure."

34. "Toads don't drink water, Winifred. It wouldn't do him any good. They take it in through their skins, like a sponge. When it rains."

35. "I don't know, but it doesn't matter. Tell your father I want to help. I have to help. If it wasn't for me, there wouldn't have been any trouble in the first place. Tell him I have to."

36. "There! You're safe. Forever."

37. "Two years. She's been gone two years."

38. "Well, where to now, Tuck? No need to come back here no more."

39. "Durn fool thing must think it's going to live forever."

LESSON SIXTEEN

Objective
1. To give students the opportunity to share Nonfiction Reading
2. To give students the opportunity to share Writing Assignments
3. To provide students with the opportunity to pursue a topic of interest to them from the Extra Activities Packet

Activity #1
Ask students to briefly summarize their findings from their nonfiction reading assignment and report them to the class.

Activity #2
Give students who would like to share any of their Writing Assignments the opportunity to read these orally or display their ads.

Activity #3
Allow students to select an activity of their choice from the Extra Activities Packet. Also encourage students to create an activity of their own that corresponds to this unit.

LESSON SEVENTEEN

Objective
To review all of the vocabulary work done in this unit

Activity
Choose one (or more) of the vocabulary review activities listed on the next page(s) and spend your class period as directed in the activity. Some of the materials for these review activities are located in the Vocabulary Resources section of this unit.

VOCABULARY REVIEW ACTIVITIES

1. Divide your class into two teams and have an old-fashioned spelling or definition bee.

2. Give each of your students (or students in groups of two, three or four) a *Tuck Everlasting* Vocabulary Word Search Puzzle. The person (group) to find all of the vocabulary words in the puzzle first wins.

3. Give students a *Tuck Everlasting* Vocabulary Word Search Puzzle without the word list. The person or group to find the most vocabulary words in the puzzle wins.

4. Use a *Tuck Everlasting* Vocabulary Crossword Puzzle. Put the puzzle onto a transparency on the overhead projector (so everyone can see it), and do the puzzle together as a class.

5. Give students a *Tuck Everlasting* Vocabulary Matching Worksheet to do.

6. Divide your class into two teams. Use the *Tuck Everlasting* vocabulary words with their letters jumbled as a word list. Student 1 from Team A faces off against Student 1 from Team B. You write the first jumbled word on the board. The first student (1A or 1B) to unscramble the word wins the chance for his/her team to score points. If 1A wins the jumble, go to student 2A and give him/her a definition. He/she must give you the correct spelling of the vocabulary word which fits that definition. If he/she does, Team A scores a point, and you give student 3A a definition for which you expect a correctly spelled matching vocabulary word. Continue giving Team A definitions until some team member makes an incorrect response. An incorrect response sends the game back to the jumbled-word face off, this time with students 2A and 2B. Instead of repeating giving definitions to the first few students of each team, continue with the student after the one who gave the last incorrect response on the team. For example, if Team B wins the jumbled-word face-off, and student 5B gave the last incorrect answer for Team B, you would start this round of definition questions with student 6B, and so on. The team with the most points wins!

7. Have students write a story in which they correctly use as many vocabulary words as possible. Have students read their compositions orally. Post the most original compositions on your bulletin board.

LESSON EIGHTEEN

Objective
    To review the main ideas presented in *Tuck Everlasting*

Activity #1
    Choose one of the review games/activities included in the packet and spend your class period as outlined there. Some materials for these activities are located in the Unit Resources section of this unit.

Activity #2
    Remind students that the Unit Test will be in the next class meeting. Stress the review of the Study Guides and their class notes as a last minute, brush-up review for the unit test.

REVIEW GAMES/ACTIVITIES - *Tuck Everlasting*

1. Ask the class to make up a unit test for *Tuck Everlasting*. The test should have 4 sections: matching, true/false, short answer, and essay. Students may use 1/2 period to make the test and then swap papers and use the other 1/2 class period to take a test a classmate has devised (open book). You may want to use the unit test included in this packet or take questions from the students' unit tests to formulate your own test.

2. Take 1/2 period for students to make up true and false questions (including the answers). Collect the papers and divide the class into two teams. Draw a big tic-tac-toe board on the chalk board. Make one team X and one team O. Ask questions to each side, giving each student one turn. If the question is answered correctly, that students' team's letter (X or O) is placed in the box. If the answer is incorrect, no mark is placed in the box. The object is to get three marks in a row like tic-tac-toe. You may want to keep track of the number of games won for each team.

3. Take 1/2 period for students to make up questions (true/false and short answer). Collect the questions. Divide the class into two teams. You'll alternate asking questions to individual members of teams A & B (like in a spelling bee). The question keeps going from A to B until it is correctly answered, then a new question is asked. A correct answer does not allow the team to get another question. Correct answers are +2 points; incorrect answers are -1 point.

4. Have students pair up and quiz each other from their study guides and class notes.

5. Give students a *Tuck Everlasting* crossword puzzle to complete.

6. Divide your class into two teams. Use the *Tuck Everlasting* crossword words with their letters jumbled as a word list. Student 1 from Team A faces off against Student 1 from Team B. You write the first jumbled word on the board. The first student (1A or 1B) to unscramble the word wins the chance for his/her team to score points. If 1A wins the jumble, go to student 2A and give him/her a clue. He/she must give you the correct word which matches that clue. If he/she does, Team A scores a point, and you give student 3A a clue for which you expect another correct response. Continue giving Team A clues until some team member makes an incorrect response. An incorrect response sends the game back to the jumbled-word face off, this time with students 2A and 2B. Instead of repeating giving clues to the first few students of each team, continue with the student after the one who gave the last incorrect response on the team. For example, if Team B wins the jumbled-word face-off, and student 5B gave the last incorrect answer for Team B, you would start this round of clue questions with student 6B, and so on.

UNIT TESTS

SHORT ANSWER UNIT TEST 1 - *Tuck Everlasting*

I. Matching/Identify

____ 1. PEBBLES   A. Given in exchange for Winnie's rescue

____ 2. RAIN   B. Spurts the fountain of youth

____ 3. WOOD   C. Tucks did this to Winnie

____ 4. STUCK   D. Winnie's childhood

____ 5. LIGHTNING   E. Author

____ 6. OVERPROTECTED   F. Flashed when window came out

____ 7. ANGUS   G. Hated being stuck in time

____ 8. ASH   H. Winnie's age

____ 9. TEN YEARS   I. How Tucks return to Treegap after seventy years

____ 10. HORSE   J. Owned the wood

____ 11. BLANKET   K. Gave a bottle of spring water to Winnie

____ 12. IRON FENCE   L. Time between visits by Tuck's sons

____ 13. TEN   M. How Angus described them

____ 14. FOSTERS   N. Center of universe

____ 15. SPRING   O. Surrounds touch-me-not cottage

____ 16. JESSE   P. Stolen by stranger

____ 17. KIDNAPPED   Q. Stacked up to hide spring

____ 18. WHEEL   R. Winnie wrapped up in to fool constable

____ 19. BUGGY   S. Began when Mae got out of window

____ 20. BABBITT   T. Giant tree in the center of the wood

Tuck Everlasting Short Answer Unit Test 1 Page 2

II. Short Answer

1. Describe the touch-me-not cottage.

2. What lies at the center of the wood?

3. For how many years had all the Tucks remained exactly the same?

4. What does Winnie Foster tell a toad at noon the same day and why?

5. Why did Winnie's grandmother become so excited when she heard music coming from the wood?

6. What does Winnie want to do that the boy refuses to allow her to do?

7 How was Winnie's kidnapping different from her imagined one?

8. When did the Tucks realize there was something peculiar about themselves and their horse?

9. What conclusion did the Tucks draw concerning their changelessness?

Tuck Everlasting Short Answer Unit Test 1 Page 3

10. Who secretly overheard the entire Tuck story?

11. Why does Angus take Winnie out in the rowboat on the pond?

12. What suggestion does Jesse make to Winnie?

13. How have Winnie's feelings changed about the Tucks?

14. How did the stranger come to know of the "ageless" family?

15. Explain the stranger's plan for the wood.

16. How does Winnie protect the Tucks when the constable accuses them of kidnapping?

17. Why does Winnie think Mae Tuck can't be hanged?

18. How does Winnie offer to help the Tucks?

19. How did Winnie's status change with her peers because of the incident?

Tuck Everlasting Short Answer Unit Test 1 page 4

20. Why does Mae state in the Epilogue they have no need to come back to Treegap?

III. Essay
    Both Winnie and Miles wanted to do something important and make a difference in the world. Did they? Support your opinion with references from the novel.

IV. Vocabulary
    Listen to the vocabulary words and spell them. After you have spelled all the words, go back and write down the definitions.

1.

2.

3.

4.

5.

6.

7.

8.

9.

10.

KEY: SHORT ANSWER UNIT TEST #1 - *Tuck Everlasting*

I. Matching/Identify

Q - 1. PEBBLES   A. Given in exchange for Winnie's rescue

S - 2. RAIN   B. Spurts the fountain of youth

A - 3. WOOD   C. Tucks did this to Winnie

M - 4. STUCK   D. Winnie's childhood

F - 5. LIGHTNING   E. Author

D - 6. OVERPROTECTED   F. Flashed when window came out

G - 7. ANGUS   G. Hated being stuck in time

T - 8. ASH   H. Winnie's age

L - 9. TEN YEARS   I. How Tucks return to Treegap after seventy years

P - 10. HORSE   J. Owned the wood

R - 11. BLANKET   K. Gave a bottle of spring water to Winnie

O - 12. IRON FENCE   L. Time between visits by Tuck's sons

H - 13. TEN   M. How Angus described them

J - 14. FOSTERS   N. Center of universe

B - 15. SPRING   O. Surrounds touch-me-not cottage

K - 16. JESSE   P. Stolen by stranger

C - 17. KIDNAPPED   Q. Stacked up to hide spring

N - 18. WHEEL   R. Winnie wrapped up in to fool constable

I - 19. BUGGY   S. Began when Mae got out of window

E - 20. BABBITT   T. Giant tree in the center of the wood

II. Short Answer

1. Describe the touch-me-not cottage.
    It was a square and solid cottage with a touch-me-not appearance surrounded by grass cut painfully to the quick and enclosed by a capable iron fence some four feet high which clearly said "Move on-we don't want you here." It was so proud of itself that you wanted to make a lot of noise as you passed, maybe even throw a rock or two.

2. What lies at the center of the wood?
    A giant ash tree lies at the center of the wood with a bubbling spring among its roots with a pile of pebbles piled there to conceal it.

3. For how many years had all the Tucks remained exactly the same?
    For eighty-seven years they had all remained exactly the same.

4. What does Winnie Foster tell a toad at noon the same day and why?
    She wants to be by herself for a change. She wants to do something that would make some kind of difference in the world. She wants to run away from home because she is closely watched by her parents and grandfather with very little freedom.

5. Why did Winnie's grandmother become so excited when she heard music coming from the wood?
    She thinks it is the elf music she had heard long ago. She had told Winnie stories about it.

6. What does Winnie want to do that the boy refuses to allow her to do?
    She wants to take a drink from the little spring from which she saw him drinking.

7. How was Winnie's kidnaping different from her imagined one?
    Her kidnappers appeared as alarmed as she was.

8. When did the Tucks realize there was something peculiar about themselves and their horse?
    They realized something wasn't right when potentially harmful events didn't affect them.

9. What conclusion did the Tucks draw concerning their changelessness?
    They decided that the source of their changelessness was the spring they had drunk from in the wood. The cat had not drunk from it and had died ten years earlier.

10. Who secretly overheard the entire Tuck story?
    The man in the yellow suit had crept up in the bushes and heard the entire fascinating story.

11. Why does Angus take Winnie out in the rowboat on the pond?

    He wants to explain to her the cycle of life as compared to the cycle of the water's life. He wants her to understand how horrible it really is to be outside of the cycle and STUCK like the Tucks. He stresses how dangerous it would be for others to discover the spring.

12. What suggestion does Jesse make to Winnie?

    He asks her to wait six years, when she will be his age, and then drink from the spring. They can then marry, see the world, and have a grand time.

13. How have Winnie's feelings changed about the Tucks?

    She loves this peculiar family and feels that they belong to her.

14. How did the stranger come to know of the "ageless" family?

    His grandmother had told him wild, unbelievable stories of an "odd" family. A dear friend of hers had married into this family and she and her two children had come to live with his grandmother for awhile. The tune from Mae's music box had been a clue, when the stranger had heard it at the Foster's gate he knew he was close to finding them.

15. Explain the stranger's plan for the wood.

    He plans to sell the water.

16. How does Winnie protect the Tucks when the constable accuses them of kidnapping?

    She tells him that they didn't kidnap her, she went with them because she wanted to.

17. Why does Winnie think Mae Tuck can't be hanged?

    She would not be able to hanged because they can't die.

18. How does Winnie offer to help the Tucks?

    She tells Jesse she will take Mae's place in the jailhouse after they get Mae out of the window, so they can get further away before the constable realizes his prisoner is gone.

19. How did Winnie's status change with her peers because of the incident?

    They were impressed by what she had done. She was a figure of romance to them now. They came by to look at her and to talk to her through the fence. Before she had been too clean to be a real friend.

20. Why does Mae state they have no need to come back to Treegap?

    They find Winnie's tombstone in the family plot at the local cemetery.

III. Essay

Both Winnie and Miles wanted to do something important and make a difference in the world. Did they? Support your opinion with references from the novel.

Answers will vary. You need to grade these according to your own criteria.

IV. Vocabulary

Choose ten of the vocabulary words to read orally for the vocabulary section of this unit test.

SHORT ANSWER UNIT TEST 2 - *Tuck Everlasting*

I. Matching/Identify

____ 1. BARN-RED   A. Winnie went fishing in this

____ 2. BLANKET   B. Began when Mae got out of window

____ 3. TEN   C. Arrested Mae

____ 4. WOOD   D. Crawled through the jailhouse window

____ 5. ROWBOAT   E. Jesse's age

____ 6. RIFLE   F. Winnie's age

____ 7. BUGGY   G. Winnie wrapped up in to fool constable

____ 8. PEBBLES   H. Number of years since the jailhouse escape

____ 9. RAIN   I. Stacked up to hide spring

____ 10. WINNIE FOSTER   J. Time between visits by Tuck's sons

____ 11. SEVENTY   K. Town near the wood

____ 12. MAE   L. Given in exchange for Winnie's rescue

____ 13. KIDNAPPED   M. Hated being stuck in time

____ 14. LIVE-LONG YEAR   N. Begun when the Tucks drank from the spring

____ 15. SEVENTEEN   O. How Tucks return to Treegap after seventy years

____ 16. CONSTABLE   P. Became a hero among her peers

____ 17. TEN YEARS   Q. Color of Tuck's home

____ 18. WOODEN TOYS   R. Angus and Mae made to sell

____ 19. TREEGAP   S. Tucks did this to Winnie

____ 20. ANGUS   T. Mae hit stranger with this

Tuck Everlasting Short Answer Unit Test 2 Page 2

II. Short Answer

1. Which month is at the top of the live-long year?

2. What item does Mae take along with her when she went to meet her sons?

3. Describe the stranger who appears at the Foster's gate at sunset of the same day.

4. What does Winnie see in the wood?

5. What does Winnie want to do that the boy refuses to allow her to do?

6. What calmed Winnie's sobbing?

7. When did the Tucks realize there was something peculiar about themselves and their horse?

8. What conclusion did the Tucks draw concerning their changelessness?

9. Who secretly overheard the entire Tuck story?

Tuck Everlasting Short Answer Unit Test 2 Page 3

10. Describe the Tuck homeplace.

11. How is the Tuck home different from what Winnie is used to?

12. What suggestion does Jesse make to Winnie?

13. What is the man in the yellow suit asking as a trade from the Fosters for the return of their daughter?

14. How did the stranger come to know of the "ageless" family?

15. Explain the stranger's plan for the wood.

16. What does Mae do that surprises everyone?

17. How does Winnie offer to help the Tucks?

18. How did the constable react when he found out about the switch?

Tuck Everlasting Short Answer Unit Test 2 Page 4

19. Explain what Winnie does to the toad and why.

20. What do the Tucks learn happened to the wood, tree, and spring?

III. Essay
    Were the Tucks "good" people? Why or why not? Cite examples and support from the novel.

Tuck Everlasting Short Answer Unit Test 2 Page 5

IV. Vocabulary

Listen to the vocabulary words and spell them. After you have spelled all the words, go back and write down the definitions.

1.

2.

3.

4.

5.

6.

7.

8.

9.

10.

KEY: SHORT ANSWER UNIT TEST 2 - *Tuck Everlasting*

I. Matching

Q - 1. BARN-RED		A. Winnie went fishing in this
G - 2. BLANKET		B. Began when Mae got out of window
F - 3. TEN		C. Arrested Mae
L - 4. WOOD		D. Crawled through the jailhouse window
A - 5. ROWBOAT		E. Jesse's age
T - 6. RIFLE		F. Winnie's age
O - 7. BUGGY		G. Winnie wrapped up in to fool constable
I - 8. PEBBLES		H. Number of years since the jailhouse escape
B - 9. RAIN		I. Stacked up to hide spring
P - 10. WINNIE FOSTER		J. Time between visits by Tuck's sons
H - 11. SEVENTY		K. Town near the wood
D - 12. MAE		L. Given in exchange for Winnie's rescue
S - 13. KIDNAPPED		M. Hated being stuck in time
N - 14. LIVE-LONG YEAR		N. Begun when the Tucks drank from the spring
E - 15. SEVENTEEN		O. How Tucks return to Treegap after seventy years
C - 16. CONSTABLE		P. Became a hero among her peers
J - 17. TEN YEARS		Q. Color of Tuck's home
R - 18. WOODEN TOYS		R. Angus and Mae made to sell
K - 19. TREEGAP		S. Tucks did this to Winnie
M - 20. ANGUS		T. Mae hit stranger with this

II. Short Answer

1. Which month is at the top of the live-long year?
    The first week of August hangs at the very top of the live-long year.

2. What item did Mae take along with her when she went to meet her sons?
    She took the one pretty thing she owned: her music box, painted with roses and lilies of the valley.

3. Describe the stranger who appears at the Foster's gate at sunset of the same day.
    He was remarkably tall and narrow with a long chin that faded off into a thin, apologetic beard. His suit was a jaunty yellow that seemed to glow a little in the fading light. A black hat dangled from one hand.

4. What does Winnie see in the wood?
    She sees a thin, sunburned wonderful boy drinking from a little spring near a huge tree.

5. What does Winnie want to do that the boy refuses to allow her to do?
    She wants to take a drink from the little spring from which she saw him drinking.

6. What calmed Winnie's sobbing?
    She ceased sobbing after Mae started her music box.

7. When did the Tucks realize there was something peculiar about themselves and their horse?
    They realized something wasn't right when potentially harmful events didn't affect them.

8. What conclusion did the Tucks draw concerning their changelessness?
    They decided that the source of their changelessness was the spring they had drunk from in the wood. The cat had not drunk from it and had died ten years earlier.

9. Who secretly overheard the entire Tuck story?
    The man in the yellow suit had crept up in the bushes and heard the entire fascinating story.

10. Describe the Tuck homeplace.
    Their barn-red homely little house sits in a deep hollow below which is a tiny lake.

11. How is the Tuck home different from what Winnie is used to?
    She has been trained to keep absolute order and their home was pleasantly cluttered and is in a state of disarray.

12. What suggestion does Jesse make to Winnie?
    He asks her to wait six years, when she will be his age, and then drink from the spring. They can then marry, see the world, and have a grand time.

13. What is the man in the yellow suit asking as a trade from the Fosters for the return of their daughter?
    He wants to own the wood; signed over to him legally.

14. How did the stranger come to know of the "ageless" family?
    His grandmother had told him wild, unbelievable stories of an "odd" family. A dear friend of hers had married into this family and she and her two children had come to live with his grandmother for awhile. The tune from Mae's music box had been a clue, when the stranger had heard it at the Foster's gate he knew he was close to finding them.

15. Explain the stranger's plan for the wood.
    He plans to sell the water.

16. What does Mae do that surprises everyone?
    She hit the stranger in the back of his skull with the stock of Angus' shotgun.

17. How does Winnie offer to help the Tucks?
    She tells Jesse she will take Mae's place in the jailhouse after they get Mae out of the window, so they can get further away before the constable realizes his prisoner is gone.

18. How did the constable react when he found out about the switch?
    He became very angry and called her a criminal and an accomplice. He released her into the custody of her parents because of her age,

19. Explain what Winnie did to the toad and why.
    She poured the precious water from the spring that Jesse had given to her over the toad so he would not have to be harmed by the dog. She wanted to protect him.

20. What do the Tucks learn happened to the wood, tree, and spring?
    They discover there was a big electrical storm. The big tree got hit by lightning, caught fire and had to be bulldozed out. All sign of the spring was gone.

III. Essay

Were the Tucks "good" people? Why or why not? Cite examples and support from the novel. Grade this essay according to your own criteria.

IV. Vocabulary

Choose ten of the vocabulary words to read orally for the vocabulary section of the test.

1.

2.

3.

4.

5.

6.

7.

8.

9.

10.

ADVANCED SHORT ANSWER UNIT TEST - *Tuck Everlasting*

I. Matching

_____ 1. BARN-RED   A. Winnie went fishing in this

_____ 2. BLANKET   B. Began when Mae got out of window

_____ 3. TEN   C. Arrested Mae

_____ 4. WOOD   D. Crawled through the jailhouse window

_____ 5. ROWBOAT   E. Jesse's age

_____ 6. RIFLE   F. Winnie's age

_____ 7. BUGGY   G. Winnie wrapped up in to fool constable

_____ 8. PEBBLES   H. Number of years since the jailhouse escape

_____ 9. RAIN   I. Stacked up to hide spring

_____ 10. WINNIE FOSTER   J. Time between visits by Tuck's sons

_____ 11. SEVENTY   K. Town near the wood

_____ 12. MAE   L. Given in exchange for Winnie's rescue

_____ 13. KIDNAPPED   M. Hated being stuck in time

_____ 14. LIVE-LONG YEAR   N. Begun when the Tucks drank from the spring

_____ 15. SEVENTEEN   O. How Tucks return to Treegap after seventy years

_____ 16. CONSTABLE   P. Became a hero among her peers

_____ 17. TEN YEARS   Q. Color of Tuck's home

_____ 18. WOODEN TOYS   R. Angus and Mae made to sell

_____ 19. TREEGAP   S. Tucks did this to Winnie

_____ 20. ANGUS   T. Mae hit stranger with this

Tuck Everlasting Advanced Short Answer Unit Test Page 2

II. Short Answer

1. Why do you think the toad was introduced to the story?

2. Explain the significance of the title "*Tuck Everlasting*".

3. Were the Tucks "good" people? Why or why not?

4. What did you learn from the story of *Tuck Everlasting?*

5. Why was the small town called Treegap?

Tuck Everlasting Advanced Short Answer Unit Test Page 3

6. Evaluate the stranger's plan for the spring.

7. Explain what these lines from an old poem on page 123 mean , "Stone walls do not a prison make, Nor iron bars a cage."

III. Quotations: Explain the importance and meaning of the following quotations.

1. "Believe me, Winnie Foster, it would be terrible for you if you drank any of this water. Just terrible. I can't let you."

2. "Well, boys, here it is. The worst is happening at last."

3. "Pa thinks it's something left over from-well, from some other plan for the way the world should be, some plan that didn't work out too good. And so everything was changed. Except that the spring was passed over, somehow or other. Maybe he's right. I don't know."

Tuck Everlasting Advanced Short Answer Unit Test Page 4

4. "It's a wheel, Winnie. Everything's a wheel, turning and turning, never stopping. Dying's part of the wheel, right there next to being born. You can't pick out the pieces you like and leave the rest. Being part of the whole thing, that's the blessing."

5. "The way I see it, it's no good hiding yourself away, like Pa and lots of other people. And it's no good just thinking of your own pleasure, either. People got to do something useful if they're going to take up space in the world."

6. "People got to be meat-eaters sometimes, though. It's the natural way. And that means killing things."

7. "Freaks. You want us to be freaks. In a patent-medicine show."

8. "They'd all come running like pigs to slop."

9. "Durn fool thing must think it's going to live forever."

Tuck Everlasting Advanced Short Answer Unit Test Page 5

IV. Vocabulary

Listen to the vocabulary words and write them down. After you have written down all the words, write a paragraph in which you use all the words. The paragraph must in some way relate to *Tuck Everlasting*.

MULTIPLE CHOICE UNIT TEST 1 - *Tuck Everlasting*

I. Matching

____ 1. RAINBOW TROUT   A. Stranger wants to do this to spring water

____ 2. MIDNIGHT   B. Miles threw back because of Winnie

____ 3. JAIL   C. Gave a bottle of spring water to Winnie

____ 4. SELL   D. Center of universe

____ 5. SEVENTY   E. Number of years Tucks remained unchanged

____ 6. WOOD   F. Angus and Mae made to sell

____ 7. YELLOW SUIT   G. Miles removed from window

____ 8. EIGHTY-SEVEN   H. Crawled through the jailhouse window

____ 9. MAE   I. Winnie took Mae's place there

____ 10. TOUCH-ME-NOT   J. The Foster's cottage

____ 11. WHEEL   K. Worn by the stranger

____ 12. JESSE   L. Mae's philosophy

____ 13. NAILS   M. Number of years since the jailhouse escape

____ 14. ONE DAY AT A TIME   N. Given in exchange for Winnie's rescue

____ 15. WOODEN TOYS   O. Meeting time for Jesse and Winnie

Tuck Everlasting Multiple Choice Unit Test 1 page 2

II. Multiple Choice

1. The month at the top of the live-long year is
    a. January
    b. December
    c. August
    d. none of the above

2. What lies at the center of the wood?
    a. an ash tree
    b. a pebble- covered spring
    c. both a and b

3. Describe the stranger who appears at the Foster's gate at sunset of the same day.
    a. He was remarkably tall with a round chin.
    b. He was tall and wore a yellow suit.
    c. He wore a black hat and had a thick mustache.
    d. He was tall and lanky with a light- colored suit and hat.

4. When she is in the wood, Winnie first sees
    a. a bubbling spring partially hidden by a stack of pebbles.
    b. a broken-down horse resting after its journey.
    c. a young brown- haired boy wearing green suspenders.
    d. a young curly-headed boy dressed in an elf suit.

5. Winnie's kidnapping is similar to what she imagined it would be like.
    a. true
    b. false

6. Mae is able to calm Winnie's sobbing by
    a. hugging her close to herself.
    b. explaining that they are harmless and will take her home soon.
    c. winding up the music box and letting it play its melody.
    d. reassuring her the wood and the spring.

7. The Tucks realized they were different from normal people when
    a. their cat died a natural death.
    b. they were not harmed by potentially harmful events.
    c. Miles wife left and took the children.
    d. none of the above

Tuck Everlasting Multiple Choice Unit Test 1 page 3

8. Angus Tuck's reaction upon his family bringing Winnie home with them is one of
    a. fear.
    b. elation.
    c. confusion.
    d. frustration.

9. Angus takes Winnie out in the rowboat after dinner to
    a. explain the danger of the spring water.
    b. use the water as an example of the cycle of life.
    c. express his frustration at being stuck in the life process.
    d. all of the above

10. Jesse suggests to Winnie that she
    a. run away with him for a grand time.
    b. tell her parents why she left home.
    c. go fishing with him in the morning.
    d. drink from the spring when she is his age, marry him, and stay that age forever with him.

11. What do Miles and Winnie have in common?
    a. Neither of them like to kill animals.
    b. They both are allergic to certain foods.
    c. They both are unhappy with how their parents treat them.
    d. Both want to do something important; to make a difference.

12. After Miles throws the rainbow trout back in the pond he tells Winnie
    a. that sometimes you have to kill; it's the natural way of things.
    b. his family wil be sore because they were expecting fish for breakfast.
    c. she will come to like the looks of fish after awhile.
    d. he doesn't like to keep them either, they are too much trouble to clean.

13. The man in the yellow suit learned of the "ageless" family through
    a. watching and waiting for them.
    b. his grandmother's friend.
    c. the music of Mae's music box.
    d. none of the above

Tuck Everlasting Multiple Choice Unit Test 1 page 4

14. When the stranger tried to take Winnie away against her will, Mae
    a. shot him with Angus' shotgun.
    b. hit him with the stock of Angus' rifle.
    c. grabbed Winnie away from him.
    d. cried for help from the approaching constable.

15. The Foster's reaction upon Winnie's homecoming was one of:
    a. fear, anxiety, and cheer.
    b. delight, anger, and curiosity.
    c. excitement, fretting, and relief.
    d. hysteria, question, punishment.

16. Winnie offers to help the Tucks out by
    a. taking Mae's place in the jailhouse.
    b. coming to their house and fixing the meals.
    c. vowing never to speak of the spring to a living soul.
    d. agreeing to destroy the spring as soon as possible.

17. Select the set of adjectives that best describes Winnie's feelings in prior to leaving to meet Jesse.
    a. restless, excited, guilty
    b. scared, excited, angry
    c. thrilled, tired, worried
    d. fearful, nervous, anxious

18. Were Winnie's school friends *more* or *less* attracted to her after this incident?
    a. more
    b. less

19. Winnie protects the toad by
    a. taking it into her house and putting it in a cage with some grass.
    b. chasing the dog away.
    c. asking her grandmother for a stick to scare away the cat.
    d. pouring the bottled spring water over it.

20. Mae and Angus learn that
    a. Winnie died two years ago from the inscription on the tombstone.
    b. the wood burned down from an electrical storm.
    c. the spring had been bulldozed away.
    d. all of the above

Tuck Everlasting Multiple Choice Unit Test 1 page 5

III. Quotations: Identify the speaker:

A= Jesse B= Grandmother C= Stranger D= Angus E= Miles

F= Mae G= Constable H=Winnie

1. "Why should you have to be cooped up in a cage, too? It'd be better if I could be like you, out in the open and making up my own mind. Do you know they hardly ever let me out of this yard all by myself? I'll never be able to do anything important if I stay in here like this. I expect I better run away."

2. "Did you hear that Winifred? That's it! That's the elf music I told you about. Why, it's been ages since I heard it last. And this is the first time you've ever heard it, isn't it? Wait till we tell your father."

3. "Believe me, Winnie Foster, it would be terrible for you if you drank any of this water. Just terrible. I can't let you."

4. "Well, boys, here it is. The worst is happening at last."

5. "Pa thinks it's something left over from-well, from some other plan for the way the world should be, some plan that didn't work out too good. And so everything was changed. Except that the spring was passed over, somehow or other. Maybe he's right. I don't know."

6. "Tuck and me, we got each other, and that's a lot. The boys, now, they go their separate ways. They're some different, don't always get on too good. But they come home whenever the spirit moves, and every ten year, first week of August, they meet at the spring and come home together.

7. "Life. Moving, growing changing, never the same two minutes together. This water, you look out at it every minute, and it looks the same, but it ain't. All night long it's been moving, coming in through the stream back there to the west, slipping out through the stream down east here, always quiet, always new, moving on. You can't hardly see the current, can you? And sometimes the wind makes it look like it's going the other way. But it's always there, the water's always moving on, and someday, after a long while, it comes to the ocean."

8. "Can you picture what that means? Forever? The wheel would keep on going round, the water rolling by to the ocean, but the people would've turned into nothing but rocks by the side of the road. 'Cause they wouldn't know till after, and then it'd be too late. Do you see now child?"

Tuck Everlasting Multiple Choice Unit Test 1 page 6

9. "How'd it be if you was to wait till you're seventeen, same as me- heck that's only six years off- and then you could go and drink some, and then you could go away with me! We could get married, even."

10. "Now, I don't have to spell things out for people like yourselves. Some types one comes across can't seem to cut their way through any problem, and that does make things difficult. But you, I don't have to explain the situation to you. I've got what you want, and you've got what I want. Of course, you might find that child without me, but...you might not find her in time. So: I want the wood and you want the child. It's a trade. A simple, clear-cut trade."

11. "The way I see it, it's no good hiding yourself away, like Pa and lots of other people. And it's no good just thinking of your own pleasure, either. People got to do something useful if they're going to take up space in the world."

12. "People got to be meat-eaters sometimes, though. It's the natural way. And that means killing things."

13. "Hear me out. As I've told you, I was fascinated by my grandmother's stories. People who never grew older! It was fantastic. It took possession of me. I decided to devote my life to finding out if it could be true, and if so, how and why."

14. "Not Winnie! You ain't going to do a thing like that to Winnie. And you ain't going to give out the secret."

15. "Yep, she got him a good one, all right. He never even come to. So it's an open-and-shut case, since I seen her do it. Eyewitness. No question about it. They'll hang her for sure."

Tuck Everlasting Multiple Choice Unit Test 1 page 7

IV. Vocabulary (Matching)

____ 1. MEAGER		A. comfortingly; soothingly
____ 2. TEEMING		B. disapproval of self
____ 3. REVOLUTIONARY		C. bustling; swarming
____ 4. MELANCHOLY		D. branch of science
____ 5. GALLOWS		E. departure
____ 6. RECEDED		F. worn out; exhausted
____ 7. ENVIOUS		G. calm; peaceful
____ 8. TANGENT		H. rebellious; unique
____ 9. GALLING		I. skimpy; sparse
____ 10. CAVERNOUS		J. dull; dreary
____ 11. METAPHYSICS		K. gloomy; woeful
____ 12. PROSTRATE		L. sorrowfully
____ 13. TRANQUIL		M. hollow and deep sounding
____ 14. SELF-DEPRECATION		N. hanging structure
____ 15. PONDEROUS		O. burden; trial
____ 16. PLAINTIVELY		P. crossness; irritability
____ 17. PETULANCE		Q. amazing; remarkable
____ 18. EXTRAORDINARY		R. annoying; irritating
____ 19. ORDEAL		S. jealous; resentful
____ 20. CONSOLINGLY		T. lessened; subsided

MULTIPLE CHOICE UNIT TEST 2 - *Tuck Everlasting*

I. Matching

____ 1. STUCK   A. Winnie's childhood

____ 2. KIDNAPPED   B. How Angus described them

____ 3. EIGHTY-SEVEN   C. Hated being stuck in time

____ 4. OVERPROTECTED   D. Number of years since the jailhouse escape

____ 5. JAIL   E. Top of the live-long year

____ 6. AUGUST   F. Winnie took Mae's place there

____ 7. IRON FENCE   G. Jesse's age

____ 8. MUSIC BOX   H. Mae's prettiest possession

____ 9. SEVENTEEN   I. Surrounds touch-me-not cottage

____ 10. ANGUS   J. Number of years Tucks remained unchanged

____ 11. CAT   K. Winnie poured over toad

____ 12. BLEW OVER   L. This happened to gallows during storm

____ 13. PEBBLES   M. Tucks did this to Winnie

____ 14. SEVENTY   N. Died a natural death

____ 15. BOTTLED WATER   O. Stacked up to hide spring

Tuck Everlasting Multiple Choice Unit Test 2 page 2

II. Multiple Choice

1. The touch-me-not cottage seemed to say
    a. "Move on-we don't want you here."
    b. "Welcome one and all."
    c. " Go away and don't come back."
    d. " Please don't pick the daisies."

2. Why did the wood 'make you want to speak in whispers'?
    a. It was spooky due to the large, dark pine trees.
    b. The darkness scared the animals and made them quiet.
    c. The trees were so tall and dark.
    d. It had a sleeping appearance.

3. When Mae leaves for her journey, she takes
    a. a music box painted with roses and lilies of the valley.
    b. the old family horse.
    c. the one pretty thing she owns.
    d. all of the above

4. The Tucks have not changed for
    a. seventy years.
    b. sixty-five years.
    c. seventeen years.
    d. eighty- seven years.

5. What does Winnie Foster tell a toad at noon the same day?
    a. She wants to be by herself for a change.
    b. She wants to do something that would make some kind of difference in the world.
    c. She wants to run away from home.
    d. all of the above

6. Why does Winnie want to do this?
    a. She is closely watched constantly by her parents and grandfather with very little freedom.
    b. She reads lots of adventure books and has a vivid imagination.
    c. She is tired of never seeing her relatives who live in on the other side of the wood.
    d. She wants to change the world for the better because her parents encourage her to do it.

Tuck Everlasting Multiple Choice Unit Test 2 page 3

7. The stranger is looking for
    a. the lost tree and spring.
    b. Winnie's father, who owed the wood.
    c. a certain family he thought lived nearby.
    d. a friendly toad that he has been following.

8. Winnie wants to
    a. drink from the flowing stream.
    b. know where from where the stranger has come.
    c. be able to leave home whenever she wants
    d. drink from the bubbling water.

9. The Tucks realized they were different from normal people when
    a. their cat died a natural death.
    b. they were not harmed by potentially harmful events.
    c. Miles wife left and took the children.
    d. none of the above

10. The Tucks came to the conclusion that
    a. the spring was the source of their agelessness.
    b. they were crazy.
    c. their cat was luckier than they.
    d. the T carved in the ash tree had not changed either.

11. Unbeknownest to Winnie, Mae, Jesse, and Miles; who overheard their entire unbelievable story?
    a. the Fosters
    b. the constable
    c. the man in the yellow suit
    d. Angus

12. The Tuck home is
    a. painted barn-red and has a tiny lake near it.
    b. deeper in the wood, past the spring.
    c. a yellow clapboard house in a clearing.
    d. none of the above

Tuck Everlasting Multiple Choice Unit Test 2 page 4

13. The main difference between the Foster house and the Tuck's is
    a. the style in which they eat their meals.
    b. the way they greet each other.
    c. the lack of overall organization and order.
    d. the openness with which they share their feelings.

14. During dinner at the Tuck's Winnie
    a. gets a tummy ache and has to lie down.
    b. becomes homesick as her spirits drop.
    c. is amused at the Tuck's lack of manners.
    d. has a fit of hysterics and can't be settled.

15. Angus takes Winnie out in the rowboat after dinner to
    a. explain the danger of the spring water.
    b. use the water as an example of the cycle of life.
    c. express his frustration at being stuck in the life process.
    d. all of the above

16. The man in the yellow suit is asking
    a. directions to the Tuck household.
    b. Angus for permission to fish on his pond.
    c. for the wood to be signed over to him in return for Winnie.
    d. Winnie to come to Treegap with him for a church picnic.

17. After Miles throws the rainbow trout back in the pond he tells Winnie
    a. that sometimes you have to kill; it's the natural way of things.
    b. his family wil be sore because they were expecting fish for breakfast.
    c. she will come to like the looks of fish after awhile.
    d. he doesn't like to keep them either, they are too much trouble to clean.

18. What is the stranger's plan for the wood?
    a. He has an idea for a town park.
    b. He wants to build a set of new cottages.
    c. He plans to sell the water.
    d. He wants the Tucks to work for him running the ferris wheel.

Tuck Everlasting Multiple Choice Unit Test 2 page 5

19. Winnie told the constable that the Tucks did not kidnap her; she went with them willingly.
    a. true
    b. false

20. Winnie knows that Mae must not be hanged because
    a. she will not be there to help her family.
    b. she loves her too much.
    c. she is not guilty of any wrongdoing.
    d. she can't die

III. Quotations: Identify the speaker:

A= Miles   B= Grandmother   C= Stranger   D= Angus   E=Mae

F= Jesse   G= Winnie   H= Constable

1. "Why should you have to be cooped up in a cage, too? It'd be better if I could be like you, out in the open and making up my own mind. Do you know they hardly ever let me out of this yard all by myself? I'll never be able to do anything important if I stay in here like this. I expect I better run away."

2. "Did you hear that Winifred? That's it! That's the elf music I told you about. Why, it's been ages since I heard it last. And this is the first time you've ever heard it, isn't it? Wait till we tell your father."

3. "Believe me, Winnie Foster, it would be terrible for you if you drank any of this water. Just terrible. I can't let you."

4. "Well, boys, here it is. The worst is happening at last."

5. "Pa thinks it's something left over from-well, from some other plan for the way the world should be, some plan that didn't work out too good. And so everything was changed. Except that the spring was passed over, somehow or other. Maybe he's right. I don't know."

6. "Tuck and me, we got each other, and that's a lot. The boys, now, they go their separate ways. They're some different, don't always get on too good. But they come home whenever the spirit moves, and every ten years, first week of August, they meet at the spring and come home together.

Tuck Everlasting Multiple Choice Unit Test 2 page 6

7. "Life. Moving, growing changing, never the same two minutes together. This water, you look out at it every minute, and it looks the same, but it ain't. All night long it's been moving, coming in through the stream back there to the west, slipping out through the stream down east here, always quiet, always new, moving on. You can't hardly see the current, can you? And sometimes the wind makes it look like it's going the other way. But it's always there, the water's always moving on, and someday, after a long while, it comes to the ocean."

8. "Can you picture what that means? Forever? The wheel would keep on going round, the water rolling by to the ocean, but the people would've turned into nothing but rocks by the side of the road. 'Cause they wouldn't know till after, and then it'd be too late. Do you see now child?"

9. "How'd it be if you was to wait till you're seventeen, same as me- heck that's only six years off- and then you could go and drink some, and then you could go away with me! We could get married, even."

10. "Now, I don't have to spell things out for people like yourselves. Some types one comes across can't seem to cut their way through any problem, and that does make things difficult. But you, I don't have to explain the situation to you. I've got what you want, and you've got what I want. Of course, you might find that child without me, but...you might not find her in time. So: I want the wood and you want the child. It's a trade. A simple, clear-cut trade."

11. "The way I see it, it's no good hiding yourself away, like Pa and lots of other people. And it's no good just thinking of your own pleasure, either. People got to do something useful if they're going to take up space in the world."

12. "People got to be meat-eaters sometimes, though. It's the natural way. And that means killing"

13. "Hear me out. As I've told you, I was fascinated by my grandmother's stories. People who never grew older! It was fantastic. It took possession of me. I decided to devote my life to finding out if it could be true, and if so, how and why."

14. "Not Winnie! You ain't going to do a thing like that to Winnie. And you ain't going to give out the secret."

15. "Yep, she got him a good one, all right. He never even come to. So it's an open-and-shut case, since I seen her do it. Eyewitness. No question about it. They'll hang her for sure."

Tuck Everlasting Multiple Choice Unit Test 2 page 7

IV. Vocabulary (Matching)

____ 1. GALLING   A. calmly

____ 2. PERIL   B. disapproval of self

____ 3. METAPHYSICS   C. thrashing

____ 4. ELATED   D. annoying; irritating

____ 5. PARSON   E. in a 'beside the point' manner

____ 6. GENTILITY   F. pain; suffering

____ 7. TRANQUIL   G. without regret

____ 8. RUEFUL   H. ecstatic; thrilled

____ 9. GANDER   I. branch of science

____ 10. FLAILING   J. to bring out of a state of sleep

____ 11. IRRELEVANTLY   K. rebellious; unique

____ 12. SELF-DEPRECATION   L. mournful; pitiful

____ 13. EXULTANT   M. minister; preacher

____ 14. SEDATELY   N. calm; peaceful

____ 15. SELF-ASSURANCE O. confidence

____ 16. REMORSELESS   P. elegance; grace

____ 17. REVOLUTIONARY Q. overjoyed; happy

____ 18. DECISIVELY   R. look

____ 19. ANGUISH   S. with determination

____ 20. ROUST   T. danger

ANSWER SHEET - *Tuck Everlasting*
Multiple Choice Unit Tests

I. Matching
1. ___
2. ___
3. ___
4. ___
5. ___
6. ___
7. ___
8. ___
9. ___
10. ___
11. ___
12. ___
13. ___
14. ___
15. ___

II. Multiple Choice
1. (A) (B) (C) (D)
2. (A) (B) (C) (D)
3. (A) (B) (C) (D)
4. (A) (B) (C) (D)
5. (A) (B) (C) (D)
6. (A) (B) (C) (D)
7. (A) (B) (C) (D)
8. (A) (B) (C) (D)
9. (A) (B) (C) (D)
10. (A) (B) (C) (D)
11. (A) (B) (C) (D)
12. (A) (B) (C) (D)
13. (A) (B) (C) (D)
14. (A) (B) (C) (D)
15. (A) (B) (C) (D)
16. (A) (B) (C) (D)
17. (A) (B) (C) (D)
18. (A) (B) (C) (D)
19. (A) (B) (C) (D)
20. (A) (B) (C) (D)

III. Quotes
1. (A) (B) (C) (D) (E) (F) (G) (H)
2. (A) (B) (C) (D) (E) (F) (G) (H)
3. (A) (B) (C) (D) (E) (F) (G) (H)
4. (A) (B) (C) (D) (E) (F) (G) (H)
5. (A) (B) (C) (D) (E) (F) (G) (H)
6. (A) (B) (C) (D) (E) (F) (G) (H)
7. (A) (B) (C) (D) (E) (F) (G) (H)
8. (A) (B) (C) (D) (E) (F) (G) (H)
9. (A) (B) (C) (D) (E) (F) (G) (H)
10. (A) (B) (C) (D) (E) (F) (G) (H)
11. (A) (B) (C) (D) (E) (F) (G) (H)
12. (A) (B) (C) (D) (E) (F) (G) (H)
13. (A) (B) (C) (D) (E) (F) (G) (H)
14. (A) (B) (C) (D) (E) (F) (G) (H)
15. (A) (B) (C) (D) (E) (F) (G) (H)

V. Vocabulary
1. ___
2. ___
3. ___
4. ___
5. ___
6. ___
7. ___
8. ___
9. ___
10. ___
11. ___
12. ___
13. ___
14. ___
15. ___
16. ___
17. ___
18. ___
19. ___
20. ___

ANSWER SHEET KEY - *Tuck Everlasting*
Multiple Choice Unit Test 1

I. Matching
1.   B
2.   O
3.   I
4.   A
5.   M
6.   N
7.   K
8.   E
9.   H
10.   J
11.   D
12.   C
13.   G
14.   L
15.   F

II. Multiple Choice
1. (A) (B) ( ) (D)
2. (A) (B) ( ) (D)
3. (A) ( ) (C) (D)
4. (A) (B) (C) ( )
5. (A) ( ) (C) (D)
6. (A) (B) ( ) (D)
7. (A) ( ) (C) (D)
8. (A) ( ) (C) (D)
9. (A) (B) (C) ( )
10. (A) (B) (C) ( )
11. (A) (B) (C) ( )
12. ( ) (B) (C) (D)
13. (A) ( ) (C) (D)
14. (A) ( ) (C) (D)
15. (A) (B) ( ) (D)
16. ( ) (B) (C) (D)
17. ( ) (B) (C) (D)
18. ( ) (B) (C) (D)
19. (A) (B) (C) ( )
20. (A) (B) (C) ( )

III. Quotes
1. (A) (B) (C) (D) (E) (F) (G) ( )
2. (A) ( ) (C) (D) (E) (F) (G) (H)
3. ( ) (B) (C) (D) (E) (F) (G) (H)
4. (A) (B) (C) (D) (E) ( ) (G) (H)
5. ( ) (B) (C) (D) (E) (F) (G) (H)
6. (A) (B) (C) (D) (E) ( ) (G) (H)
7. (A) (B) (C) ( ) (E) (F) (G) (H)
8. (A) (B) (C) ( ) (E) (F) (G) (H)
9. ( ) (B) (C) (D) (E) (F) (G) (H)
10. (A) (B) ( ) (D) (E) (F) (G) (H)
11. (A) (B) (C) (D) ( ) (F) (G) (H)
12. (A) (B) (C) (D) ( ) (F) (G) (H)
13. (A) (B) ( ) (D) (E) (F) (G) (H)
14. (A) (B) (C) (D) (E) ( ) (G) (H)
15. (A) (B) (C) (D) (E) (F) ( ) (H)

V. Vocabulary
1.   I
2.   C
3.   H
4.   K
5.   N
6.   T
7.   S
8.   E
9.   R
10.   M
11.   D
12.   F
13.   G
14.   B
15.   J
16.   L
17.   P
18.   Q
19.   O
20.   A

ANSWER SHEET KEY - *Tuck Everlasting*
Multiple Choice Unit Test 2

I. Matching
1. B
2. M
3. J
4. A
5. F
6. E
7. I
8. H
9. G
10. C
11. N
12. L
13. O
14. D
15. K

II. Multiple Choice
1. ( ) (B) (C) (D)
2. (A) (B) (C) ( )
3. (A) (B) (C) ( )
4. (A) (B) (C) ( )
5. (A) (B) (C) ( )
6. ( ) (B) (C) (D)
7. (A) (B) ( ) (D)
8. (A) (B) (C) ( )
9. (A) ( ) (C) (D)
10. ( ) (B) (C) (D)
11. (A) (B) ( ) (D)
12. ( ) (B) (C) (D)
13. (A) (B) ( ) (D)
14. (A) ( ) (C) (D)
15. (A) (B) (C) ( )
16. (A) (B) ( ) (D)
17. ( ) (B) (C) (D)
18. (A) (B) ( ) (D)
19. ( ) (B) (C) (D)
20. (A) (B) (C) ( )

III. Quotes
1. (A) (B) (C) (D) (E) (F) ( ) (H)
2. (A) ( ) (C) (D) (E) (F) (G) (H)
3. (A) (B) (C) (D) (E) ( ) (G) (H)
4. (A) (B) (C) (D) ( ) (F) (G) (H)
5. (A) (B) (C) (D) ( ) (F) (G) (H)
6. (A) (B) (C) (D) ( ) (F) (G) (H)
7. (A) (B) (C) ( ) (E) (F) (G) (H)
8. (A) (B) (C) ( ) (E) (F) (G) (H)
9. (A) (B) (C) (D) (E) ( ) (G) (H)
10. (A) (B) ( ) (D) (E) (F) (G) (H)
11. ( ) (B) (C) (D) (E) (F) (G) (H)
12. ( ) (B) (C) (D) (E) (F) (G) (H)
13. (A) (B) ( ) (D) (E) (F) (G) (H)
14. (A) (B) (C) (D) ( ) (F) (G) (H)
15. (A) (B) (C) (D) (E) (F) (G) ( )

V. Vocabulary
1. D
2. T
3. I
4. Q
5. M
6. P
7. N
8. L
9. R
10. C
11. E
12. B
13. H
14. A
15. O
16. G
17. K
18. S
19. F
20. J

UNIT RESOURCE MATERIALS

BULLETIN BOARD IDEAS - *Tuck Everlasting*

1. Create a large calendar for the first week of August only, to match the story's timeline- the start of the live-long year. Illustrate with hot weather activities.

2. Bring in (or have students bring in) pictures of fresh water springs, wheels, ferris wheels, woods, toads, rainbow trout, music boxes, cottages, horses, jails, gallows, (1880's) etc. Make a collage if you have enough different pictures (or post individual pictures on colorful paper if you only have a few pictures). This could also be a fun introductory activity if students participate. You could have the border and title done for the bulletin board and invite students to staple up their own pictures wherever they want them. It will only take a few minutes of class time, but the students will enjoy it and you can get your bulletin board done in a hurry.

3. Draw one of the word search puzzles onto the bulletin board. (Be sure to enlarge it.) Write the key words to one side. Invite students to take their pens or markers and find the words before and/or after class (or perhaps this could be an activity for students who finish their work early).

4. Make an enlargement of Mae's music box. Have students do research in the novel for an exact description.

5. Illustrate Winnie and Jesse by either silhouettes, portraits, or whatever your choice. Include information gained from the novel describing them.

6. Post words of the old poem Winnie thinks of when Mae is trying to get out of jailhouse. Post students' interpretation of it.

7. Make a mural depicting Treegap, the Tuck homeplace, and the wood; including the tree and spring.

8. Post any of the students' Writing Assignments. They could illustrate something from their Writing Assignment to enhance it.

9. Create a collage of art work from students that conveys their impressions of the characters in this story.

10. Portray the Tuck and Foster families. Make two separate family portraits and display. Each character could be described as well.

11. Post an illustration of a large ferris wheel. Have students label the different seats with items that revolve around one center. (i.e. individual class names with class title in center, etc.)

EXTRA ACTIVITIES - *Tuck Everlasting*

One of the difficulties in teaching a novel is that all students don't read at the same speed. One student who likes to read may take the book home and finish it in a day or two. Sometimes a few students finish the in-class assignments early. The problem, then, is finding suitable extra activities for students.

One thing you can do is to keep a little library in the classroom. For this unit on *Tuck Everlasting*, you might check out from the school library other books by Natalie Babbitt. A biography of the author would be interesting for some students. You may include other related books and articles about: everlasting life, the fountain of youth, 1880's small towns, ferris wheels, music boxes, kidnappings, toads, life cycles, etc.

Other things you may keep on hand are puzzles. We have made some relating directly to *Tuck Everlasting* for you. Feel free to duplicate them for your students.0

Some students may like to draw. You might devise a contest or allow some extra-credit grade for students who draw characters or scenes from *Tuck Everlasting*. Note, too, that if the students do not want to keep their drawings you may pick up some extra bulletin board materials this way. If you have a contest and you supply the prize or, you could possibly make the drawing itself a non-refundable entry fee.

The pages which follow contain games, puzzles and worksheets. The keys, when appropriate, immediately follow the puzzle or worksheet. There are two main groups of activities: one group for the unit; that is, generally relating to the *Tuck Everlasting* text, and another group of activities related strictly to the *Tuck Everlasting* vocabulary.

Directions for the games, puzzles and worksheets are self-explanatory. The object here is to provide you with extra materials you may use in any way you choose.

MORE ACTIVITIES - *Tuck Everlasting*

1. Pick a chapter or scene with a great deal of dialogue and have the students act it out on a stage. (Perhaps you could assign various scenes to different groups of students so more than one scene could be acted and more students could participate.)

2. Discuss the concept of land ownership as mentioned on page 7 of the novel. Have students ask an authority from local government to explain the laws on it. Perhaps interview a surveyor to discuss this topic.

3. Students could write epitaphs for Winnie. Include her most important accomplishments.

4. Debate the effects of overprotectiveness. Debate the pros and cons of everlasting life.

5. Use some of the related topics (noted earlier for an in-class library) as topics for research, reports or written papers, or as topics for guest speakers.

6. Have students plan and teach a lesson on a chapter or section of the book. Give them guidelines and a timeframe.

7. Visit a fair or carnival that has a ferris wheel.

8. Integrate with science and/or social studies on the life cycle of living things and of water as discussed by Tuck with Winnie in the rowboat. Make posters illustrating what students have learned.

9. Write to Natalie Babbitt asking her questions students have composed. You could send a class set of letters in one large envelope.

10. Construct a model of the center of the wood including the tree and spring.

11. Research music boxes. Have a music box day where students bring in a favorite one and share.

12. Allow students to select a character from the novel. Have them dress like them, speak like them; assume their persona. Create a talk show format with these characters as the guests. Have a student volunteer to be the host. Others not involved will the audience, questioning the characters. One of your students could pretend to be a trained psychologist who comes out later in the show to help the panel solve their problems. Have a topic like: overprotectiveness, i.e. problems encountered in the novel. Allow the class to decide as much as possible. Have questions from the audience ready prior to the show day. You could have students try out for the parts. Remind them to keep it on the up and up, not to mimic some of the seedier talk shows. This will require students to take an in-depth look into characterization in the novel.

More Activities - *Tuck Everlasting* page 2

13. View a filmstrip on Natalie Babbitt, if available.

14. Students who like board games may want to create one using information from this novel. Some students could work together as a group to complete this task. Encourage them to look at setting to illustrate their board and possibly use vocabulary, characters, plot, etc. for question cards.

15. Do a study on kidnapping. Chart results.

16. Research the practice of hanging (1880's).

17. Make or display some wooden utensils or toys, such as Mae and Angus made to sell. Discover how much work would it take to create these things.

18. Invite a carpenter in to your class to discuss and maybe demonstrate how hard or easy it would be to actually remove a window from a structure, like Miles did at the jailhouse.

19. Read some other fantasies and compare to this one.

20. Research toads and present information to the class. Perhaps have a few live ones on hand.

21. Hold a mock trial for the man in the yellow suit's murder.

22. Discuss why the Tucks moved on constantly. List why modern people choose to move on today. Compare the reasons.

23. View the video version of *Tuck Everlasting*. Compare the book and the movie.

PROJECT

The Treegap Times

Project The Treegap Times is an optional project included in this unit. Students will work on this independently on their own time outside of class. If so inclined, you may choose to change these requirements to meet your specific students' needs.

Activity #1

    Tell students that they will be creating a newspaper for the Treegap community, the setting of their novel. Before they begin, have them examine a variety of newspapers to get the feel for the different columns and their contents.

Activity #2

    After students have a good idea what typical newspapers are like, have them elect an editor and assistant editor. Remind them that an editor must be knowledgeable about punctuation, spelling and good usage. They must also be able to take charge without being bossy. You may also want them to elect a production manager to be in charge of the layout.

Activity #3

    Allow students to decide on the sections that will appear in their paper. They might include front-page news (Woman Breaks Out of Jail!), editorials, letters to the editor, weather, births, deaths, advice column, comics, advertisements, classified, sports, entertainment, fashions, food, gossip, etc. Give students a chance to select the section on which they would like to work. Determine how many reporters are needed for each section by the overall size of your class.

Activity #4

    Give students guidelines for reporting and deadlines for the final product. Remind them to refer to the text for ideas on what to report. Allow what class time you can spare to be spent how the editors and production manager see fit. Allow students to determine media, pictures, size, type of paper to be used, etc. Have fun!

WORD SEARCH - Tuck Everlasting

```
R N W E L B J T A S H N P Y T O Y S J Y J
O A A N M L N A D U O E R G H N V T E S H
W I T C I A R F I R G T D G G E Z R S L K
B L E C L C K I I L N U J U I T K A S A L
O S R F E K Z W F E B N S B N W S N E N Y
A S P S S M O G P L R A E T D E T G L N C
T S R P W D E R K A E N I S I N U E B A W
H O U R N T A T B F C G L W M T C R A W C
H R A I N C R D E A M U F I D Y K L T I J
R V W N T A A E L R B S E M E D Y N S N D
G D Q G E O V P V S Y D R T V W P U N Q
P V Q Y T H X P E B C B I R I B M Y O I C
S E V E N T Y A S C A H F O L K T W C E M
G E W M Q X B N C U T B T U S H R H O C W
D B V C B J L D W R J G B T G Q E E B O Y
Z K T E D D A I C S D Y D I B X E E S F D
K X O F N P N K G E P G E R T W G L N W T
G Q U Y O T K P Q H V O R T D T A V Y B Z
G Q C G J S E G E T T L N T S D P D B K P
D B H B G D T E L B V N S D X Q N S Y N L
F B V K V R J E N F B W I Z N B C X D M S
P S T C Q Z F Q R P D L B N Q F V K P D N
G X F H D X N S F S Y V E W G Q X M T B W
X C W Y D J Y Y G K B S T S T W X P T N W
```

ANGUS	DEVIL	NAILS	TEN
ANNA	EIGHTY	ONE	TOAD
ASH	ELVES	PEBBLES	TOUCH
AUGUST	FIREFLIES	POND	TOYS
BABBITT	FOSTERS	RAIN	TREEGAP
BARN	HORSE	RIFLE	TROUT
BLACK	IRON	ROWBOAT	TWENTY
BLANKET	JAIL	SELL	WATER
BLEW	JESSE	SEVENTEEN	WHEEL
BUGGY	KIDNAPPED	SEVENTY	WINDOW
CARPENTRY	LIGHTNING	SPRING	WINNIE
CAT	MAE	STRANGER	WOOD
CEMETERY	MIDNIGHT	STUCK	YEAR
CONSTABLE	MILES	SUIT	
CURSE	MUSIC	SWIM	

WORD SEARCH ANSWER KEY - Tuck Everlasting

ANGUS	DEVIL	NAILS	TEN
ANNA	EIGHTY	ONE	TOAD
ASH	ELVES	PEBBLES	TOUCH
AUGUST	FIREFLIES	POND	TOYS
BABBITT	FOSTERS	RAIN	TREEGAP
BARN	HORSE	RIFLE	TROUT
BLACK	IRON	ROWBOAT	TWENTY
BLANKET	JAIL	SELL	WATER
BLEW	JESSE	SEVENTEEN	WHEEL
BUGGY	KIDNAPPED	SEVENTY	WINDOW
CARPENTRY	LIGHTNING	SPRING	WINNIE
CAT	MAE	STRANGER	WOOD
CEMETERY	MIDNIGHT	STUCK	YEAR
CONSTABLE	MILES	SUIT	
CURSE	MUSIC	SWIM	

CROSSWORD - *Tuck Everlasting*

CROSSWORD CLUES - *Tuck Everlasting*

ACROSS
2. What boys do when they get home
6. Top of the live-long year
8. Owned the wood
9. Mae hit stranger with this
11. Hated being stuck in time
12. Sight organ
13. Giant tree in the center of the wood
15. Winnie's age
17. Miles' wife thought he sold his soul to him
19. Began when Mae got out of window
20. Grandma thought they made the music
21. How Tucks return to Treegap after seventy years
22. Myself
23. Stranger wants to do this to spring water
27. Everlasting amphibian
28. Winnie took Mae's place there
30. Center of universe
34. Light ____ or tulip ____
35. Also
36. Spurts the fountain of youth
38. Tuck household
39. Winnie went fishing in this

DOWN
1. Gave a bottle of spring water to Winnie
2. Wore a yellow suit
3. Crawled through the jailhouse window
4. Endless life to Angus
5. Wished to do something important
7. Town near the wood
8. Winnie liked to catch these
10. Mae's prettiest possession
13. Miles' daughter
14. Stolen by stranger
16. Worn by the stranger
18. Number of years Tucks remained unchanged
24. Died a natural death
25. Worn by the yellow suited man
26. Stacked up to hide spring
29. Coordinating conjunction meaning also
31. How Angus described them
32. Explains the cycle of life
33. Miles removes from the jail
37. Given in exchange for Winnie's rescue

CROSSWORD ANSWER KEY - *Tuck Everlasting*

MATCHING QUIZ/WORKSHEET 1 - *Tuck Everlasting*

____ 1. ELVES   A. Begun when the Tucks drank from the spring

____ 2. STRANGER   B. Miles removed from window

____ 3. SWIM   C. Given in exchange for Winnie's rescue

____ 4. IRON FENCE   D. Time between visits by Tuck's sons

____ 5. CAT   E. Wore a yellow suit

____ 6. JAIL   F. Jesse's age

____ 7. TREEGAP   G. What boys do when they get home

____ 8. WOOD   H. Owned the wood

____ 9. TOAD   I. Mae hit stranger with this

____ 10. RIFLE   J. This happened to gallows during storm

____ 11. NAILS   K. Flashed when window came out

____ 12. LIVE-LONG YEAR   L. Surrounds touch-me-not cottage

____ 13. BLANKET   M. Winnie took Mae's place there

____ 14. BLEW OVER   N. Town near the wood

____ 15. YELLOW SUIT   O. Miles' age

____ 16. LIGHTNING   P. Winnie wrapped up in to fool constable

____ 17. TEN YEARS   Q. Grandma thought they made the music

____ 18. SEVENTEEN   R. Died a natural death

____ 19. FOSTERS   S. Everlasting amphibian

____ 20. TWENTY-TWO   T. Worn by the stranger

KEY: MATCHING QUIZ/WORKSHEET 1 - *Tuck Everlasting*

Q - 1. ELVES   A. Begun when the Tucks drank from the spring

E - 2. STRANGER   B. Miles removed from window

G - 3. SWIM   C. Given in exchange for Winnie's rescue

L - 4. IRON FENCE   D. Time between visits by Tuck's sons

R - 5. CAT   E. Wore a yellow suit

M - 6. JAIL   F. Jesse's age

N - 7. TREEGAP   G. What boys do when they get home

C - 8. WOOD   H. Owned the wood

S - 9. TOAD   I. Mae hit stranger with this

I - 10. RIFLE   J. This happened to gallows during storm

B - 11. NAILS   K. Flashed when window came out

A - 12. LIVE-LONG YEAR   L. Surrounds touch-me-not cottage

P - 13. BLANKET   M. Winnie took Mae's place there

J - 14. BLEW OVER   N. Town near the wood

T - 15. YELLOW SUIT   O. Miles' age

K - 16. LIGHTNING   P. Winnie wrapped up in to fool constable

D - 17. TEN YEARS   Q. Grandma thought they made the music

F - 18. SEVENTEEN   R. Died a natural death

H - 19. FOSTERS   S. Everlasting amphibian

O - 20. TWENTY-TWO   T. Worn by the stranger

MATCHING QUIZ/WORKSHEET 2 - *Tuck Everlasting*

____ 1. BARN-RED   A. Winnie went fishing in this

____ 2. BLANKET   B. Began when Mae got out of window

____ 3. TEN   C. Arrested Mae

____ 4. WOOD   D. Crawled through the jailhouse window

____ 5. ROWBOAT   E. Jesse's age

____ 6. RIFLE   F. Winnie's age

____ 7. BUGGY   G. Winnie wrapped up in to fool constable

____ 8. PEBBLES   H. Number of years since the jailhouse escape

____ 9. RAIN   I. Stacked up to hide spring

____ 10. WINNIE FOSTER   J. Time between visits by Tuck's sons

____ 11. SEVENTY   K. Town near the wood

____ 12. MAE   L. Given in exchange for Winnie's rescue

____ 13. KIDNAPPED   M. Hated being stuck in time

____ 14. LIVE-LONG YEAR   N. Begun when the Tucks drank from the spring

____ 15. SEVENTEEN   O. How Tucks return to Treegap after seventy years

____ 16. CONSTABLE   P. Became a hero among her peers

____ 17. TEN YEARS   Q. Color of Tuck's home

____ 18. WOODEN TOYS   R. Angus and Mae made to sell

____ 19. TREEGAP   S. Tucks did this to Winnie

____ 20. ANGUS   T. Mae hit stranger with this

KEY: MATCHING QUIZ/WORKSHEET 2 - *Tuck Everlasting*

Q - 1. BARN-RED	A. Winnie went fishing in this
G - 2. BLANKET	B. Began when Mae got out of window
F - 3. TEN	C. Arrested Mae
L - 4. WOOD	D. Crawled through the jailhouse window
A - 5. ROWBOAT	E. Jesse's age
T - 6. RIFLE	F. Winnie's age
O - 7. BUGGY	G. Winnie wrapped up in to fool constable
I - 8. PEBBLES	H. Number of years since the jailhouse escape
B - 9. RAIN	I. Stacked up to hide spring
P - 10. WINNIE FOSTER	J. Time between visits by Tuck's sons
H - 11. SEVENTY	K. Town near the wood
D - 12. MAE	L. Given in exchange for Winnie's rescue
S - 13. KIDNAPPED	M. Hated being stuck in time
N - 14. LIVE-LONG YEAR	N. Begun when the Tucks drank from the spring
E - 15. SEVENTEEN	O. How Tucks return to Treegap after seventy years
C - 16. CONSTABLE	P. Became a hero among her peers
J - 17. TEN YEARS	Q. Color of Tuck's home
R - 18. WOODEN TOYS	R. Angus and Mae made to sell
K - 19. TREEGAP	S. Tucks did this to Winnie
M - 20. ANGUS	T. Mae hit stranger with this

JUGGLE LETTER REVIEW GAME CLUE SHEET - *Tuck Everlasting*

SCRAMBLED	WORD	CLUE
ATC	CAT	Died a natural death
RNERTACYP	CARPENTRY	Miles' vocation
-OCUOMENT-TH	TOUCH-ME-NOT	The Foster's cottage
DHNTGMII	MIDNIGHT	Meeting time for Jesse and Winnie
UESRC	CURSE	Endless life to Angus
ODWO	WOOD	Given in exchange for Winnie's rescue
ACOENTLBS	CONSTABLE	Arrested Mae
EOAIAETYANMTD	ONEDAYATATIME	Mae's philosophy
USYTLEWLOI	YELLOWSUIT	Worn by the stranger
LSEVE	ELVES	Grandma thought they made the music
YRCEMETE	CEMETERY	Where Tucks discover Winnie's fate
VLIED	DEVIL	Miles' wife thought he sold his soul to him
ILAJ	JAIL	Winnie took Mae's place there
RESHO	HORSE	Stolen by stranger
ESLL	SELL	Stranger wants to do this to spring water
WAROTOB	ROWBOAT	Winnie went fishing in this
EYHEG-ETSNIV	EIGHTY-SEVEN	Number of years Tucks unchanged
EYOOTDNSWO	WOODENTOYS	Angus and Mae made to sell
ANAN	ANNA	Miles' daughter
IRLEIFSEF	FIREFLIES	Winnie liked to catch these
NIAR	RAIN	Began when Mae got out of window
ANRDBR-E	BARN-RED	Color of Tuck's home
IREFL	RIFLE	Mae hit stranger with this
RYENSETA	TENYEARS	Time between visits by Tucks' sons
DOIWNW	WINDOW	Miles removes from the jail
ONDP	POND	Explains the cycle of life
CBHKLTAA	BLACKHAT	Worn by the yellow suited man
VYESENT	SEVENTY	Number of years since the jailhouse escape

Juggle Letter Review Game Clues Continued

REGRSTAN	STRANGER	Wore a yellow suit
GINLGHTIN	LIGHTNING	Flashed when window came out
PYRNAERCT	CARPENTRY	Miles' vocation
TTLWTDBREOAE	BOTTLEDWATER	Winnie poured over toad
HAS	ASH	Giant tree in the center of the wood
ELEHW	WHEEL	Center of the universe

VOCABULARY RESOURCE MATERIALS

VOCABULARY WORD SEARCH - *Tuck Everlasting*

All the words in this list are associated with *Tuck Everlasting* with emphasis on the vocabulary words being studied in the unit. The words are placed backwards, forward, diagonally, up and down. The included words are listed below the word search.

```
G E N T I L I T Y L E S R E V R E P Z K N P B V
T A E X U L T A N T U K Z R U S L L T R V S H L
W A N C A V E R N O U S Y E U A T S O T W S I J
D T N D C Z T A R E E R F O I P Y L D O I U R L
D Z L G E E I E T T A U I N Y L R L L U Q R S G
V Q G T E R D T A N L V T R T O E L G N E Y C D
P D X M A N E R I P N I A S F L A N A N L F E Q
M D I B O N T D E E V N A L B G A R I H O D W R
V N R P O S R R C E O H S A U F T V C P E N N T
G A B I O O I N L I G S T E L X O N P C Y G E S
B L R R A L A Y T S B I T A D B U R E W J S S G
N A P R O L P U T M M I I F L A E R D Z N R A H
M O T U U Q L O L O N L D A T S T E I E Q L Q T
Z X S T D O O H D I I I E S S L T E M O L K S P
E S E R V H W N F N R D X I S A J M L I U U W M
A P P E A L I N G C R E V U L S I O N Y O S F L
Q Z R C F P I D A O J E P E M E A G E R Q M W Q
```

ACRID	FLAILING	MARIONETTE	PROSTRATE
ANGUISH	FORLORN	MEAGER	RECEDED
APPEALING	GALLING	OPPRESSIVE	REVOLUTIONARY
BARBARIAN	GALLOWS	ORDEAL	REVULSION
BOVINE	GANDER	PARSON	ROUST
CAHOOTS	GENTILITY	PERIL	RUEFUL
CAVERNOUS	GHASTLY	PERILOUS	SEDATELY
ELATED	IMMENSE	PERVERSELY	STAUNCHLY
ENVIOUS	INDOMITABLE	PETULANCE	TANGENT
EXTRAORDINARY	INFINITE	PLAINTIVELY	TEEMING
EXULTANT	LUXURIOUS	PONDEROUS	TRANQUIL

VOCABULARY CROSSWORD - *Tuck Everlasting*

VOCABULARY CROSSWORD CLUES - *Tuck Everlasting*

ACROSS
1. Supreme; unconquerable
6. What boys do when they get home
8. Comprehend words with your eyes
9. Mae hit stranger with this
13. Began when Mae got out of window
14. Mournful; pitiful
15. Slender
18. Bitter; harsh
20. Figure with 6 equal sides; 3-D square
21. Danger
22. Tree juice
23. Calm; peaceful
27. Sleepy; cowlike
29. Giant tree in the center of the wood
30. With determination
33. Bird's body part for flying
35. Miles removed from window
36. Departure
37. Gave a bottle of spring water to Winnie
38. Hated being stuck in time
39. Grandma thought they made the music

DOWN
1. In a 'beside the point' manner
2. Burden; trial
3. Giant; huge
4. Pain; suffering
5. Elegant; rich
7. Crawled through the jailhouse window
10. Miserable; forsaken
11. Skimpy; sparse
12. Obedience; meekness
16. Gloomy; woeful
17. Heavy; stifling
19. Motel; small roadside sleeping/eating establishment
24. Pleasing; charming
25. Limitless
26. Bustling; swarming
28. Wished to do something important
29. Top of the live-long year
31. Winnie's age
32. Died a natural death
34. Stranger wants to do this to spring

VOCABULARY CROSSWORD ANSWER KEY - *Tuck Everlasting*

	I	N	D	O	M	I	T	A	B	L	E						S	W	I	M
	R		R		M		N		U											A
	R	E	A	D		M		G		X						R	I	F	L	E
	E			E		E		U		U		M		S				O		
	L		R	A	I	N		I		R	U	E	F	U	L			R		
	E			L		S		S		I		A		B			S	L	I	M
	V				E		H			O		G		M		O		O		E
	A	C	R	I	D				C	U	B	E		I		P	E	R	I	L
	N			N						S		R		S	A	P		N		A
	T	R	A	N	Q	U	I	L						S		R				N
	L		P			N		T		B	O	V	I	N	E					C
	Y		P		M		F		E				O		S		A	S	H	
		D	E	C	I	S	I	V	E	L	Y			N		S		U		O
	T		A		L		N		M			C		W	I	N	G			L
	E		L		E		I		I		S		A		V		U			Y
	N	A	I	L	S		T	A	N	G	E	N	T		J	E	S	S	E	
			N			E		G		L							T		
A	N	G	U	S				E	L	V	E	S								

150

VOCABULARY WORKSHEET 1 - *Tuck Everlasting*

____ 1. ROUST   A. calmly

____ 2. PLAINTIVELY   B. unlearned; ignorant people

____ 3. ILLITERATES   C. burden; trial

____ 4. PERVERSELY   D. to bring out of a state of sleep

____ 5. STAUNCHLY   E. confidence

____ 6. INFINITE   F. look

____ 7. SELF-ASSURANCE   G. in a 'beside the point' manner

____ 8. EXTRAORDINARY   H. thrashing

____ 9. IRRELEVANTLY   I. limitless

____ 10. GANDER   J. danger

____ 11. APPEALING   K. dangerous

____ 12. CAVERNOUS   L. with determination

____ 13. ORDEAL   M. minister; preacher

____ 14. METAPHYSICS   N. amazing; remarkable

____ 15. SEDATELY   O. sorrowfully

____ 16. PERILOUS   P. uncontrollably

____ 17. FLAILING   Q. hollow and deep sounding

____ 18. DECISIVELY   R. branch of science

____ 19. PARSON   S. pleasing; charming

____ 20. PERIL   T. loyally; faithfully

KEY: VOCABULARY WORKSHEET 1 - *Tuck Everlasting*

D - 1. ROUST		A. calmly
O - 2. PLAINTIVELY		B. unlearned; ignorant people
B - 3. ILLITERATES		C. burden; trial
P - 4. PERVERSELY		D. to bring out of a state of sleep
T - 5. STAUNCHLY		E. confidence
I - 6. INFINITE		F. look
E - 7. SELF-ASSURANCE		G. in a 'beside the point' manner
N - 8. EXTRAORDINARY		H. thrashing
G - 9. IRRELEVANTLY		I. limitless
F - 10. GANDER		J. danger
S - 11. APPEALING		K. dangerous
Q - 12. CAVERNOUS		L. with determination
C - 13. ORDEAL		M. minister; preacher
R - 14. METAPHYSICS		N. amazing; remarkable
A - 15. SEDATELY		O. sorrowfully
K - 16. PERILOUS		P. uncontrollably
H - 17. FLAILING		Q. hollow and deep sounding
L - 18. DECISIVELY		R. branch of science
M - 19. PARSON		S. pleasing; charming
J - 20. PERIL		T. loyally; faithfully

VOCABULARY WORKSHEET 2 - *Tuck Everlasting*

____ 1. TRANQUIL   A. elegant; rich

____ 2. ILLITERATES   B. lessened; subsided

____ 3. APPEALING   C. hanging structure

____ 4. RECEDED   D. bustling; swarming

____ 5. LUXURIOUS   E. dreadful; horrible

____ 6. ORDEAL   F. every which way; no pattern

____ 7. OPPRESSIVE   G. sorrowfully

____ 8. HELTER-SKELTER   H. unlearned; ignorant people

____ 9. REVOLUTIONARY   I. burden; trial

____ 10. SUBMISSION   J. mournful; pitiful

____ 11. MARIONETTE   K. calm; peaceful

____ 12. PLAINTIVELY   L. heavy; stifling

____ 13. RUEFUL   M. puppet

____ 14. TEEMING   N. branch of science

____ 15. METAPHYSICS   O. pain; suffering

____ 16. CAHOOTS   P. dull; dreary

____ 17. PONDEROUS   Q. partnership

____ 18. GHASTLY   R. rebellious; unique

____ 19. GALLOWS   S. pleasing; charming

____ 20. ANGUISH   T. obedience; meekness

KEY: VOCABULARY WORKSHEET 2 - *Tuck Everlasting*

K - 1. TRANQUIL	A. elegant; rich
H - 2. ILLITERATES	B. lessened; subsided
S - 3. APPEALING	C. hanging structure
B - 4. RECEDED	D. bustling; swarming
A - 5. LUXURIOUS	E. dreadful; horrible
I - 6. ORDEAL	F. every which way; no pattern
L - 7. OPPRESSIVE	G. sorrowfully
F - 8. HELTER-SKELTER	H. unlearned; ignorant people
R - 9. REVOLUTIONARY	I. burden; trial
T - 10. SUBMISSION	J. mournful; pitiful
M - 11. MARIONETTE	K. calm; peaceful
G - 12. PLAINTIVELY	L. heavy; stifling
J - 13. RUEFUL	M. puppet
D - 14. TEEMING	N. branch of science
N - 15. METAPHYSICS	O. pain; suffering
Q - 16. CAHOOTS	P. dull; dreary
P - 17. PONDEROUS	Q. partnership
E - 18. GHASTLY	R. rebellious; unique
C - 19. GALLOWS	S. pleasing; charming
O - 20. ANGUISH	T. obedience; meekness

VOCABULARY JUGGLE LETTER REVIEW GAME CLUES - *Tuck Everlasting*

SCRAMBLED	WORD	CLUE
ARENGD	GANDER	look
WLLGSAO	GALLOWS	hanging structure
EMNSIEM	IMMENSE	giant; huge
ISONUVE	ENVIOUS	jealous; resentful
RAEEMG	MEAGER	skimpy; sparse
RPYEVELSER	PERVERSELY	uncontrollably
NATUELTX	EXULTANT	ecstatic; thrilled
ATEYELSD	SEDATELY	calmly
APNTCLEEU	PETULANCE	crossness; irritability
DEELTA	ELATED	thrilled ; overjoyed
RLIEP	PERIL	danger
GLSYNIOCOLN	CONSOLINGLY	comfortingly; soothingly
OSTRU	ROUST	to bring out of a state of sleep
CDIAR	ACRID	bitter; harsh
UTNLIARQ	TRANQUIL	calm; peaceful
ETGNANT	TANGENT	departure
CUTLYHANS	STAUNCHLY	loyally; faithfully
TITNEOREAM	MARIONETTE	puppet
SSEEESMRROL	REMORSELESS	without regret
NOUVRLEIS	REVULSION	disgust; distaste
VRUCOESAN	CAVERNOUS	hollow and deep sounding
EIALITTSLRE	ILLITERATES	unlearned; ignorant people
UPSOIRLE	PERILOUS	dangerous
NLGAGLI	GALLING	annoying; irritating
IGSNUHA	ANGUISH	pain; suffering
CSTADPNR-OEFLEEI	SELF-DEPRECATION	disapproval of self
NRPOAS	PARSON	minister; preacher
IYINLGETT	GENTILITY	elegance; grace
IXRULOSUU	LUXURIOUS	elegant; rich
CHINLYFNGIUNL	UNFLINCHINGLY	unafraid; unhesitant
RESVIEOPSP	OPPRESSIVE	heavy; stifling
LRPEI	PERIL	danger
ITIYLEVAPNL	PLAINTIVELY	sorrowfully
GAELPIPAN	APPEALING	pleasing; charming
EMYNAOLHCL	MELANCHOLY	gloomy; woeful

www.ingramcontent.com/pod-product-compliance
Lightning Source LLC
Chambersburg PA
CBHW051410070526
44584CB00023B/3369